Hand Luggage — A Memoir in Verse

HAND LUGGAGE

A Memoir in Verse

P. K. Page

The Porcupine's Quill

Library and Archives Canada Cataloguing in Publication

Page, P.K. (Patricia Kathleen), 1916–
    Hand Luggage : a memoir in verse / by P.K. Page.

ISBN-13: 978-0-88984-288-5
ISBN-10: 0-88984-288-4

1. Page, P.K. (Patricia Kathleen), 1916– — Poetry. 2. Poets, Canadian
(English) — 20th century — Biography. 3. Poets, Canadian (English) —
20th century — Poetry. I. Title.

PS8531.A34H35 2006   C811'.54   C2006-900209-6

Published by The Porcupine's Quill, 68 Main St, Erin, Ontario NOB 1TO.
http://www.sentex.net/˜pql

Readied for the press by Stan Dragland.
Copy edited by Doris Cowan.

Represented in Canada by the Literary Press Group.
Trade orders are available from University of Toronto Press.

We acknowledge the support of the Ontario Arts Council and the Canada
Council for the Arts for our publishing program. The financial support of the
Government of Canada through the Book Publishing Industry Development
Program is also gratefully acknowledged. Thanks, also, to the Government
of Ontario through the Ontario Media Development Corporation's Ontario
Book Initiative.

Canada Council for the Arts   Conseil des Arts du Canada

Canadä

ONTARIO ARTS COUNCIL
CONSEIL DES ARTS DE L'ONTARIO

To Théa who suggested it
Arlene and Rosie who encouraged it
and others who were unsure —
good friends all.

I could give all to Time except — except
what I myself have held. But why declare
the things forbidden that while the Customs slept
I have crossed to safety with? For I am There,
And what I would not part with I have kept.

— Robert Frost

I

Calgary. The twenties. Cold and the sweet
melt of chinooks. A musical weather.
World rippling and running. World
watery with flutes. And woodwinds.
The wonder of water in that icy world.
The magic of melt. And the grief of it. Tears —
heart's hurt? heart's help?

This was the wilderness: western Canada.
Tomahawk country — teepees, coyotes,
cayuses, lariats. The land that Ontario
looked down its nose at. Nevertheless
we thought it civilized. Civilized? Semi.

Remittance men, ranchers — friends of my family —
public school failures, penniless outcasts,
bigoted bachelors with British accents.
But in my classroom, Canadian voices —
hard r's and flat a's, a prairie language —
were teaching me tolerance, telling me something.
This vocal chasm divided my childhood.
Talking across it, a tightrope talker,
corrected at home, corrected in classrooms:
wawteh, wadder — the wryness of words!

Such my preparation for a life of paradox —
a borderland being, barely belonging,
one on the outskirts, over the perimeter.

I was deceptive, full of disguises
a poet in residence, a private person
masked as a malamute — mutable, moody —
but would dance on a table, or argue the dawn up —
a jack-in-the-box, 'a jolly good sport'.
Tennis or riding — you'd only to try me.

The smell of a loose-box — of straw and manure
ammonia, saddle soap, hay, the metallic
jingle of bridles, 'Gear, tackle and trim,'
wild roses and lupins — sweetscent of the prairies.

Greys, dapples, and sorrels, bays, chestnuts and pintos —
I rode them and loved them. Their rumps were French-polished
their noses were velvet, wet velvet their mouths.
But fording a river, face into the current,
they were Poseidon's. Hooves slipping and sliding
flesh plunging and rising, they struggled and swam.

And so, I suppose, I struggled and swam
because where I was centred, what mattered, was art —
the Pre-Raphaelites, Rodin and Renoir and Rouault,
El Greco and Epstein, Picasso, Van Gogh —
I cherished them all in their cheap reproductions.

And poems. The pattern of vowels in a poem,
the clicking of consonants, cadence, and stress —
were magic and music. What matter the meaning?
The sound was the meaning — a mantra, a route
to the noumenon, not that I'd thought
that through absolute pitch I'd repattern myself.
What I'd *thought?* What I'd *felt*. For me feeling was thinking.
I thought with my heart — or so my heart thought.

II

London. The thirties. Thirst-quenching London.
All eyes, I was everywhere, taking it in.
Poured into paintings — the Blakes in the Round Room,
the Turners, Ben Nicholsons, Nashes, the blas-
phemy of Stanley Spencer's *St. Francis!*
Ecce Homo by Epstein — great God, what a God!
The press and the church up in arms at his cheek:
'How dare he!' 'A devil disguised as an artist.'
The public as critic? — Puh-lease! Wasn't *Rima*[1]
feathered and tarred? Take a look at it now!

Then Woolf and *The Waves*, like a shower of gold
from a shelf overhead, a bonanza from Zeus.
I wept from sheer joy as I stood there and read.
Her voices of children were voices from dream.
Who had written that way? Not Walpole, Millay
or even Zane Grey whom I'd read with a passion!
Or Kipling or Brooke. I was crazed by her rhythms
and dazed by her thought. Was it manna she offered?
Womanna. Don't laugh. I'd been tone-deaf to gender
and now I could hear. Or, put it another way, negative space
showed profiles where I'd seen a chalice before.
Something moved in my mind, and where once I was blind
I was sighted, or semi. A world opened up.
(I might add as P.S. that today I incline
to the chalice again. Is it hormones or mind?)

Gielgud as the Dane ... In the gods by myself
I thought I'd reached heaven. Heard Shakespeare and Shaw.
Their language, the lilt and the crash of it. School
had provided no pre-view. I listened to Bach
to Brahms and Beethoven.
                              Live music before

---

1 Epstein's sculpture of the wild girl in W.H. Hudson's *Green Mansions*.

was a military band, or the still-silent screen
where sounds from the pit — piano, violin —
helped horses to gallop and lovers to kiss.

And ballet — a breathtaking Russian Giselle
who, feet first, went crazy for love. You could see
her heart break in her dance. My heart broke in advance.

Returning at night on the rattling train
I heard only music and shot past my stop.
A child, deaf and dumb to the rumbles of Europe.
A nineteen-year-old with a passion for art.

III

And so, home. To the Maritimes. There I grew up
as a debutante. Dated. Drank rum and Coke
from a teapot at dances. Those temperance days
on the Kennebecasis. Why didn't we drown
as we dived full of gin? I suppose, drunkards' luck.

Easygoing, fun-loving, I tried to fit in
among embryo bankers and lawyers — the rich.
Almost made it, but always the hunger for art
interfered with romance. I was bored by their chat
so I acted in amateur theatre and wrote,
found potters and painters and poets, preferred
my typewriter to any boyfriend. Askance
was the glance of my parents — a goose (not a swan!)
from a duck egg? — dear birds of the air! What goes on?

(How talk of my parents? I think if we pick
our mothers and fathers, I showed a fine skill.
They were funny, encouraging, crazy a bit,
free-thinkers, both. A high-spirited pair.
Paradoxical too — my mother miscast
as a military wife. An 'original' more
aptly describes her. She said of herself,
'All my brain's in my fingers.' Her fingers' IQ
must have broken the scale. She was beautiful too
and my father adored her. I think I was four
when we bought for her birthday, my hand in his hand,
a gold watch for her wrist, and more wonderful still
a pair of silk stockings of bright peacock blue.
(I was crazy for colour. I crayoned a lot.)

My father was fearless — a daredevil (not
fast cars and wild women — we hadn't a car)
but he'd jump on a bull and hang on by its horns,
break remounts, and once, boots and all, took a dive

into fast running waters — the Elbow? the Bow? —
to save an old lady from drowning as if
it was part of his job, something everyone did.
He was also an artist — carved quarter-cut oak
with mallet and chisel and accurate hand.
My mother carved too and, between them, they joked
they had carved everything but the banisters and —
who knows what saved it?—the lavatory seat.

As I grew, they grew with me — or so it appeared —
companions and friends whom I loved to be with.
To breakfast we brought all our dreams — a bizarre
smorgasbord with our coffee — surreal as Chagall.
We played games, as a family — word games, not cards —
and charades and those games where you drew and passed on
body bits to your neighbour, who then added more.
We made speeches on topics picked out of a hat.
And we laughed — we were laughers, the lot of us — but
we talked about death and whether or not
the departed return. We all made a vow
that whoever went first would return, if we could.
(None has managed so far, although once, a close friend
who had died, reappeared in a dazzle of light
to tell me death wasn't the ending of 'life'.)

                              *

Then the war. And the world upside down in a trice.

We were sailing — a day as benign as a baby,
the river, *mirabile dictu*, a mirror,
sweet magic of water, when over the air
came a message of death. We were moored when it came
but set sail for harbour in silence. No word
or glance passed between us. All thinking dark thoughts.
Fear clutching our hearts. My father would go.
My brother, my beau, would be quick to enlist.

Beyond that? The mind boggled. No one could guess.

My father to Iceland. Top secret. And so
brief was his briefing we scrambled for books
to make sense of his posting to Iceland, forsooth!
For a war against Germany? Wonders or worse.
An emotional earthquake upshook us like 'foil'.

We moved, shut the house up, my mother and I
as if closing our lives. Took a place by the sea.
Lived for BBC broadcasts. The letters took weeks.
Was the writer alive as we read them? A thread,
hair-thin, stretched between us, a thread thoughtless speech
could snap with a word. So we chatted of tides,
of rationing — gas, sugar, coffee and tea —
to say nothing of booze. Local beer, our best bet.
We skimped on tobacco to send overseas,
knitted socks, balaclavas. I worked on a book.
The English boy, who was our war guest, and sent
to be safe in 'the colonies', poor little kid,
and neglected by parents, complained, 'In our house
we change in the evenings.' We said, 'At least wash!'
In England, war ended, he said he would go
to Eton or Harrow, I don't recall which,
like his father before him. Now, frightened, he clung
to the things he felt sure of — a structure, a scale.
Conditioning 's what we would call it today.
It is what we are stuck with until we can see
our Lilliput limits. My mummy said, No.
Or my mummy said, Yes. My daddy said, Stay.
Or my daddy said, Go. When my father said, Go,
although happy at home, I was gone. In a flash.

IV

Montreal. The forties. Calèches. The snow
as high as a house. Grey stone. The French.
And a room of one's own. Lapsang souchong for tea.
Alone but not lonely. My typewriter. Me.
And I wrote — a real writer — or such was my wish.

Is it luck, is it destiny? How to account
for the fact, knowing nobody, I could connect,
a kid from the sticks, with Abe Klein and Frank Scott,
Arthur Smith, Patrick Anderson, *Preview*,[2] the lot?
A miracle. More than a miracle, now,
looking back through the years, though I'm sure even then
it must have felt strange. I was out of my depth
but somehow they seemed to accept what I wrote
and, wonder of wonders! *my* views on *their* work.

We had twice-monthly meetings at Patrick's. The steps
that led to his place were a glacial chute.
In winter, we froze. In summer, the heat
melted all but our brains and our bones. But we met
and read in his rooms. And Patrick read reams,
all brilliant — Beowulf-cum-Barker,[3] a bit.
And he changed me. Enfranchised the painter in me.
I was flooded with images. Something got free.

Klein, when he came, pulled stars from the air.
His bilingual poem,[4] declaimed in his voice
was astonishing: 'almative', 'isle riverain'.
Dear Abe — he was modest, but modestly pleased

---

2 A literary magazine in Montreal edited by Patrick Anderson, Neufville Shaw,
   Bruce Ruddick, F.R. Scott, P.K. Page and, later, A.M. Klein.
3 George Barker, a British poet (1913–1993).
4 'Montreal'.

with the praises we poured on the *parle* of his verse.

We argued and criticized, crossed out, rewrote.
Talked of Rilke and Kafka . Of cummings and Stein.
Of syntax, orthography — not set in stone!
Less radical poets looked dull — no, not dull,
how could Lorca be dull? Or Auden or Yeats?
Less eye-catching, surely, but sometimes what's caught
by the eye is small fry. Whales sound in the deep.
Scott brought his own beer. Patrick brewed tea.
(As I've said, we were rationed — they drank it themselves.)
The rest of us went when the meeting broke up
to Murray's[5] for cocoa or Bowles'[6] for hot soup.
We walked — it was wartime. Few cars were about.

What baffles me now is how English we were.
In a francophone city, I never spoke French.
My friends, for the most part, were Anglos, and those
who were DPs,[7] spoke principally German and Czech,
and struggled with English. The mothers who came
from bomb-battered London with babies in tow
and husbands at hazard, spoke h'English of course.
There were writers and artists among them. I sat,
as a model for many, for none could afford
a professional model. Most painters are broke.

For Patrick's wife, Peggy, I posed in the nude
in an overstuffed chair. When the Selwyn House[8] boys
trailed in to be tutored by Patrick, she threw
me a blanket as cover. What could they have thought

---

5 One of a chain of restaurants that stayed open late.

6 A rubby-dub restaurant that stayed open all night.

7 Those who came to Canada to escape the war
   were called Displaced Persons or DPs.

8 A boys' private school in Montreal.

of that blanketed form in the room they walked through?
A monster? A sculpture that now and then moved?

Jori Smith, Philip Surrey and Marian Scott[9]
Gertrude Hermes[10] and Goodridge and Grier and Muhlstock[11] —
I respected their work and I bought when I could.
But Borduas's canvases commented on
a world overturned. With his *Refus Global*,[1]
which later proclaimed what his paintings portrayed,
church and state, the Establishment, shuddered and shook.
(I little then knew that one day I would choose
Cathédrale Engloutie[13] for a Canberra house.
But I'm leaping ahead. From here, looking back,
what was clearly consecutive no longer is.
Chronology's merely a temporal squint.)

Then like a mirage one on stilts appeared
who spoke my tongue with no interpreter
and when I came to walk at such a height
and match his stride and travel at his side
someone in me was born and someone died.

★

Next, politics! Poetry led me to *this!*
Conservatives, Liberals were all I had known.
Apolitical us, as the army *must* be,

---

9 Montreal painters.
10 Gertrude Hermes, a British wood engraver and sculptor
who came to Canada during the war.
11 Goodridge Roberts, Eldon Grier, Louis Muhlstock — Montreal painters.
12 An anti-religious, anti-establishment manifesto signed by sixteen artists in
Montreal in 1948.
13 A painting by Borduas made available by the Art Bank.

and pro-war, as of course I was — Father and bro
each uniformed, active, I couldn't agree
with Commies and Socialists, Anderson/Scott,
who were pacifists both, but for reasons apart.

Highest loyalty — Russia, for Commies, and she
wasn't part of the fight — yet!
                              When Hitler went in,
Holy Russia, heroic, our Mother for whom
the war was now righteous — their bull gored our cow! —
was our glorious ally. Go on! Even I,
ignoramus, with milk teeth, and one-eyed, could see
how the press, politicians, were twisting our arm
(synecdoche, here, a device I employ
to imply the collective. I could have said 'arms!')
And, believe me, the best arms were twisted. Some broke.

What force was at work? How figure it out?
Black was white, bad was good at the flick of a switch.
Whose the switch and who flicked it? The question remains
even now, even more, in the twenty-first C.
Why search for a villain? The villain is us.

Pro-underdog, always — most young people are,
and I still am, God help me — I'd thought Russia good,
high-principled, just, in apportioning wealth.
But the idea of 'fair' is so deep in our blood
it can blind us to kindliness, blind us to love.
Though in fairness, our blindness, our *Darkness at Noon*,[14]
was a solar eclipse — so no sunlight came through.

With Russia our ally, I raced to catch up
with communist theory. Karl Marx and Palm Dutt
broke my brain. I was better, as always, with art.

---

14 A book by Arthur Koestler.

Tólstoi and Turgénev; and Eisenstein and
Shostakovich, Prokofiev — what a *débauche!*
I learned nothing of history. I had a hard hat,
a bulletproof bonnet that kept me pristine,
protected from politics. Pure as a prayer.

★

My job was a joke. I worked in a vault
where blueprints for small arms were kept behind locks.
That wasn't the joke. What was funny was me
learning over again what I'd learned once before
in a store in Saint John selling pen nibs and books
with no laws about hours, no laws about pay
and a time clock to give us 'Good night' and 'Good day'.
I had learned — oh Lord, help us! — how hard people work
and that man-hours(!) and money don't match.

Then, Ibsen-inspired, I had surveyed the town.
Talked to waitresses, clerks, to see what went on.
Found none of it fair. And then once again,
in Montreal offices found the same thing —
the wages absurd for the work we put in.
Despite my disgust with the barons, despite
my anxiety over the war, underpaid,
'bare luxuries only' (Sacheverell's[15] *bon mot*)
meaning paintings and poetry, music and love,
I was happy and healthy and living headlong.
No matter the snow, it was summer all year.
We rejoiced in our riches. I rented a flat.
Bought Beethoven — mostly the final quartets.
Didn't question the future: the future was now.
J.W. Dunne[16] I had read in my teens

---

15 Sacheverell Sitwell.
16 *An Experiment with Time.*

but real research on time and the brain would appear
only twenty years later. Time/space a construct?
How sense such a singular concept? Who, me?
Not my mind, but my neurons, and 'I' went along.

I was published by *Poetry*,[17] wrote at a pace
I could envy today. And I do! And I do!
Now, sixty years later, the last of the herd,
I look back on a jam-packed and passionate life.
I was writing, in love, had a job, and good friends.
Oscar Peterson played in a dive down the street.

★

Then chaos and change. Is character made
by upheaval? and if so, pray tell me, are some
more entitled than others? The question remains.
I changed cities. Changed jobs. Lost my lover. And moved.
Again. And again. I lived in one room
in Ottawa, this wartime housing's decree,
and deprived of a phone — unless pregnant — poor me!
But thank God I was not. It was catch-as-catch-can.
And I caught. Where I could.

(Rereading 'One Art,'[18] I realize loss
is the ultimate art. And you learn it by heart.)

I worked as a writer — for filmstrips and film,
where image, imperial, reigns, and the word
is handmaiden only, but handmaidens have
to be skilled, inconspicuous, *cabochon*-cut.

I was busy enough. My first book came out —

---

17 *Poetry: A Magazine of Verse.*
18 A poem by Elizabeth Bishop.

of poems, that is, I had published before
a novel, if novel's the word for it — more
a short story stretched to book length and disowned
by me, older — not wiser. I hope I was not
just an ignorant ingenue knowing what's what.

The higher you fly, the farther you fall.
Once learned, you remember that lesson, alas.
But is flying a choice? Without wings you must walk.
While winged, unless you're an ostrich, a fowl
cluck cluck in the coop, then you try for the sky.

> War ended. A cause for rejoicing. For me
> it was hard to rejoice. My world hadn't held.

V

Then the fifties. Five tens. I was thirtyish, wed.
Not working, for once. I was married. A wife.
An astonishing word when applied to myself.
Wore a ring on my finger, reigned over a house,
had a husband who humoured me, ready-made kids.
For better or worse. Until death do us part.
Very fifties, the feel of it. Neighbouring friends
their husbands successful, dropped over for drinks.
A communal creature, with comforts, enhanced
by great acres of air, many minutes of space,
I read all Arthur's books — his Conrad, Chekhov
and his Palgrave, the one he had carried to war
as a boy of eighteen; and his Omar Khayyám
(Fitzgerald, of course), and his Flaubert and, far
more astonishing still, his *Arabian Nights* —
not the bowdlerized versions I'd known of before.

How talk about Arthur? I doubt that he'd like
much limelight. It wasn't his style. He had eyes
as blue as a glacier's. No one could lie
to such eyes, nor could anyone meeting him doubt
what he spoke was the truth as he saw it. He spoke
but rarely — regrettably — leaving a space
for me to fall headlong, and flat on my face.
But that wasn't his *plan*. Would he not have preferred
a wife less outspoken? He probably would.
Though questioned about it he swore he would not,
that a wife less outspoken would not have been me.
(Gallant, his reply! Though I know what he meant.
It was part of my 'me-ness', my quiddity, as
his 'his-ness' was silence. It made him himself.)

We moved to the country, a miracle move.
It was spring, cummings' spring, but the country had no
lame balloon men who whistled. Instead it had birds.

With binoculars, field books, I learned about birds —
about warblers, woodpeckers, vireos, wrens ...
their flight patterns, songs, where they nested and when.
Hollow bones! They are nothing but feathers and skin
bright eyes and sweet voices and small bursting hearts.

And wild flowers: the moosewood and moccasin flower,
lady's slipper and bloodroot, the indian pipe —
strange waxen white ghost of the woodlands that sent
a chill through my blood. As a child in the west
I was used to more pigment. There, paintbrushes flared
in the pale prairie grasses like vivid Sarcees,[19]
tagger(!) lilies in flames, and lupins as blue
as the sky upside down or some strange inland sea
had geared me to colour, imprinted my gaze.
West — violenter — volumetric and vast,
had shrunk me to size. There I'd learned about scale —
night skies, northern lights, nothing small about *them* —
but here in the East I somehow forgot.
A lesson unlearned is a lesson that's lost.

---

19 The Sarcees are a Dene tribe of the First Nations who live to the southwest
   of Calgary. We spent many summers camping on their lands and my father
   was a friend of Chief Starlight from whom he bought horses.

VI

Antipodes next. Do they stand on their heads,
as we thought in our childhood? A chance to find out.
So we put our possessions in storage and packed
for a new kind of life — a high dive, if you like.
Diplomacy, mercy! Decorum and dress,
formal dinners. And protocol! 'Make it your friend,'
the wife of a diplomat wisely advised.
What a mix of emotions. My mother was old
and a widow. I wondered…. To leave her behind
was a difficult hurdle.

　　　　　　We travelled by ship.
Stopped in London and Aden, Port Said, Ceylon.
Bombay — what a swindle! I didn't expect
to see India ever, had settled for not
setting foot on its soil. But six hours wouldn't do!
What a trip! It was hot. I longed for more time
in the ports where we stopped. The exotic, for me,
was strong drink and I craved it; a drop wouldn't do.
But it had to. And then, port-deprived, we were there,
though, having arrived, 'There' was 'Here', in a flash.
Astonishing, that. The centre is you.
Or so I thought then. Now I wonder a lot
is consciousness bred in the heart or the head?
Or somewhere outside us — the sun? outer space?

　　　　　　＊

Australia. June. Semi-tropics, when cold,
are freezing. We froze. For our Canberra house
we had to buy heaters and close up the vents
(builders' code) from the time when they lighted with gas!
It was 'pretty' — too pink, full of chintz and cretonne.
Our paintings looked blasphemous, blinding, among
all those ladylike pinks — *Cathédrale Engloutie*,
especially outrageous, we gave pride of place.

An adventure. Together. No network of friends
or family to lean on. Just us with the help
of the Chancellery staff (some better, some worse).
They gave me the scoop about places to shop:
one grocer, no cleaners, fresh fish to be shipped
from Sydney if needed, one chemist and no
movie theatre, no concerts — for those we must go
to Sydney or Melbourne. Much later, we did.
(Saw *The Consul*, Menotti — Australian cast —
even better, I thought, than the show in New York.)

How convey first impressions? Small sapphire-blue wrens —
bright gems — hopped about like our sparrows at home,
and glittering magpies, patchwork parakeets,
made an aviary out of our property where
daphnes, gardenias scented the air
like sherbets — as sharp as new gardening shears.
(A curious image. The cold and the sweet.
How otherwise conjure the strangeness of it?)
An assault on our senses.
                              Our house was Cape style —
red tiles and white stucco — of family size
with a bell in each room, and an intricate chart
in the kitchen to indicate which of us rang,
whether 'His Ex' or 'Her Ex' or 'His Little Ex',
as the family before us had so set it up.
'*Ex*(cellency)[20] — God's truth! Unbelievable swank!
But a fact is a fact, as Arthur would say,
and written, what's more, for the whole world to see.
Bad enough anywhere, but especially there
on that egalitarian continent where
all men are 'mates' and my master is me.

---

20 'His Excellency' was the official way of referring to an Ambassador or
High Commissioner. It was not a way they would refer to themselves!
And Her Excellency was not correct for the wife of an Ambassador and
as for Little Ex — well!

(We shan't mention the women. Whose masters were they?
those queens of the 'copper' and wood-burning stove.)

Down under. Domain of the red kangaroo
and joey her baby — one half-inch at birth
and raised in her pouch. Pouch potato? Pouch *meat*.
And the platypus. Egg-laying mammal. Its pelt
from a pussy-cat. Beak from a duck.
A stream dweller, structured from left-over parts
of flesh, fish and fowl when God's fancy ran free.
And then there was protocol! Unparalleled!

As the newest arrival, I needed to call
on the wives of the diplomats, one at a time.
Twenty minutes, no more. There was Thailand, Japan,
the Netherlands, Germany, France, the UK —
this latter a tartar who thought herself dean
of the Commonwealth countries, and even the Corps.
There was China, Brazil, Indonesia, Greece,
New Zealand and Russia, the US of A.
I called on them all. They in turn called on me.
Twenty minutes a call. It was more like a game
played by children — slow tag crossed with musical chairs.
Amusing. Their houses, their customs, the chat
we engaged in together, the quick cups of tea,
or sake or coffee — I took it all in
like a child in a pram. Like a child I could play
but alas and alack, could I do it all day?

Legitimized now, we were asked out to dine:
'Dinner. Black tie, 7.30 for 8.'
The 'dips', as they called us, took much of our time
and when 'the House'[21] sat, at their tables we met
the bachelor Ministers[22] from the hotel

---

21 The House of Parliament.

22 Cabinet Ministers.

whose wives wouldn't move from home towns to the bleak-
ness of Canberra; graziers (sheep);
Dep. Ministers (this was a government town);
and occasional profs (from the Uni, that is.)
I abbreviate here, an Australian trick —
'Meet me, darl, at the ciné. We'll eat at the caf.'

We found Aussies outspoken. Exponents of sport.
As their standard of living was measured by pools,
tennis courts, cricket pitches, they found us effete,
bespectacled, pale. To them England was home.
Any man worth his salt could eat a whole sheep.
Chop picnics a speciality. Wonderful lamb
cooked over eucalypts. Fit for a queen.
And she ate it, I'm sure, when she came on her tour —
but more of that later. I've made a great leap.

*

We travelled a lot. Perth to Melbourne by train —
five hundred dun-coloured miles, dry and flat —
hermetically sealed against heat. I had hoped
for the sounds and the smells as well as the sights.
All senses are one at some point and to be
dispossessed of the others, made sightedness less,
or so I had thought, though psychologists say
I am wrong, that it works in the opposite way.
(Synaesthetics unite! It is never too late
to unionize and demand our back pay.)

An elegant train with a personal shower,
polished shoes, morning tea, lots of time to digest
our western adventures. We went down the shaft
of a mine — gold, of course, at Kalgoorli, what else?
If a woman went into a mine, I'd been told,
she brought danger or worse to the miners, ergo
no woman could go, but I went in the cage

down to Dante's inferno, a lamp on my brow,
jammed in with the miners who jostled and joked.

I'd imagined the slag they brought up to the top
would be gold as my ring but of course it was not.
To judge by its colour, it might have been coal.
And what of the bullion reserves at Fort Knox?
Is the matter of gold and its glitter a hoax?

At dinner that night, from a newscast I heard
Dylan Thomas had died and I grieved by myself.
Our hosts little knew that a light had gone out.

*

Then Melbourne. Old buildings. A city of clubs.
Very British. The Britishest city of all!
We attended 'the Cup'.[23] Such astonishing hats
it might have been Ascot. Grey toppers. The lot.
And I noticed again, as I'd noticed before
how separate the sexes, when placing a bet
the wickets, like washrooms, read *Ladies* or *Men*.
Segregation — a serious matter, it seemed.
And here I digress for a moment, to ask
was it based upon 'mateship', that bonding of males,
a concept conceived in the Outback and now
invisibly part of their character? Viz:
The Seventeenth Doll, Summer of,[24] which we saw
on opening night. At its climax two men
walked into the sunset together. Could this
at that time have been written or, let alone played,
to packed houses on Broadway? Or London? No way.
And I hasten to say this was not a gay play.

---

23 The Melbourne Cup was the big horse race of the year.
24 A play by Ray Lawlor.

Back to Melbourne once more, where, because of 'the Cup'
all hotel rooms were full when we tried to reserve.
Whole families were in from the Outback, whole floors
put aside for their use. Arthur stayed at a club
(men only). And I — boarding school, here I come! —
spent the night on my own in a sumptuous bed
in a club (ladies only). We kissed on the step —
was the headmistress watching? Her surrogate eye
took the form of a servant. Starched apron and cap.

I found it absurd. Yet a part of me thought
how intriguing it was — two countries that shared
the same roots, the same language, that shared the same queen
and a system of parliament nearly the same
though not siblings, not cousins, not neighbours, were yet
not totally foreign. Christianity'd laid
its dead hand over both of us, thus were we wed.

Geography must have accounted for much.
The populace — white ('Yellow Peril'[25] take note,
and the abos,[26] forgive me! That's what they were called.
[I am critical now. Was I critical then?])
by temperament Latin, was racially Brit
and Texan in spirit. Thus, larger than life.
They were Brit to our mix. They were wool to our wheat.
They were south to our north and, though continent-sized,
were an island — an I-land — alone and apart.
The sun in their sky had a northerly slant.

In the gallery in Melbourne, a monstrous great maw,
I discovered such artists as Nolan, Dobell.
Saw paintings on bark (Aboriginal art)
in its basement (where else?), badly lighted and hung.

_____

25 A pejorative term for the Japanese, much in use immediately post-war.
26 A pejorative term for the aboriginals.

Cave paintings, perhaps, are the closest I come
to comparing, but even comparison can't
conceivably conjure their character or
the complexity of their technique. They were like —
but metaphor fails me and simile seems
a useless invention, unless in reverse:
they were *unlike* all art I had seen up to then,
including our paper-birch pictures incised
with deer-antler pens, by Algonquin and Cree.
Theirs were painted with brushes of twigs, human hair,
on eucalypt, naturally — what other tree?
They used ochre, sienna and charcoal and chalk
as their palette in painstaking intricate work.
They painted 'the Dreaming'[27] with cross-hatch and dot —
apparently abstract, but actually not.
Sign language perhaps, or symbolic, and seen
with vision dyslexic — all viewpoints at once.

(In Adelaide, twenty years later, I saw
an update: acrylic on canvas. Now, un-
circumscribed by the size of a gum,[28]
the paintings were bigger and brighter but not,
to my eye, any better than work done before.
They were beautiful, yes. Homogeneous? No.
And I asked myself then as I ask myself now —
when our options are wide and exceed either/or
are we paupers or princes? Deprived or enriched?
And reply: a low ceiling keeps planes on the ground.

Later on in Chiapas near San Cristobal[29]
I saw homogeneity whole, every house,

---

27 Aboriginal creation myth.

28 Gum tree, a colloquial word for eucalyptus, whose bark had been
    the Aboriginals' only canvas.

29 Mexico.

every stick, every stone, every colour of skin
rhymed or half-rhymed with the tones of the earth.
And remembering Rilke I knew in a rush
what he meant when he wrote of the creatures that lived
in the womb they'd emerged from. I shared in their bliss[30]
for a moment, no more. Life imprisonment in
so narrow a spectrum is sentence of death.)

Again I'm off track. But my consciousness can't,
looking backwards, reconjure the chain of events
in historical sequence. One's memories stored,
stashed away, who knows where, have a system unique
as a thumbprint — one triggered by tastes,
by weathers, by vague indefinable wants
and other ineffables — 'humours', I think,
is the word I am wanting for moistness and warmth
and temperament, too — for that watery self,
that ox-bowing river that rushes, dries out,
and is quickened by freshets and freakish flash floods.

                    ★

At the Barrier Reef, built by corals, we watched
coral polyps emerge; we saw Christmas-tree worms
form miniature undersea forests; bright fish
as solemn as clergy, as painted as clowns.
Giant clams that could swallow a typewriter lay
like suitcases under our feet. Smaller shells
like cowries and cones I had seen as a child
in my grandparents' house. (There, my uncles as boys,
those several Sinbads, collectors of shells
from the world's seven seas, had sorted, and named
and displayed their collection with exquisite care
in cabinets pull-taffy-coloured. [I craved

---

30 Rilke's Eighth *Duino Elegy.*

such a cabinet. I wanted it more
than anything I'd ever wanted before —
even more than shin plasters,[31] or shiny new shoes,
silver paper from cigarettes, cigarette cards.]
There were wonders undreamed of in drawer after drawer:
there were moon snails and sundials and turbans and tops,
and volutes and conches and tritons and whelks.
The names were like magic. I learned them by heart.]

We watched dressmaker ants, palest green, with green thread
sew together the leaves of the pandanus palm
that grew from the sand where we sunbathed and read.
And Arthur, pointillist, painted the *plage.*
A heavenly holiday — carefree and hot.

★

We drove to 'the Alice'[32] from Darwin. The car
a rickety Chev, its driver a dour
Australian Scot. Scorching weather. The sky
so blue it was hideous. Blueblueblueblue.
And wattle, yolk yellow, and bottle trees and
giant anthills, red earth, mirages of lakes —
was the moiré above them an ocular flaw?
The road like a ruler, the land like a plate,
the heat like a hammer. No humans in sight.

We stopped at three stations — cattle, not sheep —
their acreage equal to Belgium, and each
with hospitable hosts whose most wonderful gifts
were cool showers and clean clothing, deep shade and cold drinks!
Poinsettias blared, bougainvillea spread

---

31 Folding money worth 25 cents and greatly valued by
    Canadian children in the twenties.

32 An affectionate term for Alice Springs.

like a skin disease over the buildings — too red
its crimson, magenta and scarlet. Had green
disappeared from the planet? My eyes seemed to bleed.

Yet I loved it: the hard-riding stockmen who made
string figures from twine, who drove cattle and trimmed
their bush hats with feathers — galah, lorikeet;
the company store stocked with saddles and soap
and housewares and hardware. We each bought a hat
and watched as the 'lubras'[33] who worked in the house
chose bright cotton dresses and lollies, on tab.
I disliked the *idea* of the store but the *fact*
was quite different. Where else could they go?
No phones in that vastness of space, pre-TV
and pre-pre-computer. Their contact was one
and one only — 'the Holy' — far holier than
the saints in their niches — the Transceiver Set.[34]

It was doctor and school. Respected like God.
Not a toy but a tool. A lifeline, in truth.
We witnessed, with wonder, the discipline of
that scatter of people — two million square miles
was the area served. There were times set aside
for the doctor, the teacher, the women who longed
for a womanly word in that masculine world.

Between stations, the Outback — pure Somerset Maugham —
was filthy and frightening. Weirdos and freaks.
But the worst was no water — a foretaste of what
is ahead of us now, as I write. When I think
how a shower head bursts like a blossoming flower
when a tap is turned on but how, when it hangs dry

---

33 . Aboriginal women — possibly a pejorative term.

34 A two-way radio, set up by Flynn of the Outback, that made communication
    beween stations possible.

refusing its role (as each sweltering day
after sweltering day dragged its dreadful BO
past our noses and we dragged our dreadful BO
past the noses of others) it looks like a gun,
an evil, an impotent travesty of
the fountain of life. What a future!
                              And then
another day's drive through the drought and behold
Alice Springs, the miraculous! Citrus fruit trees
(a poem by Marvell) the oranges bright,
and the lemons like lamps in their glistening leaves.
How luscious a world that knows water. We washed
in it, wallowed — a sponge with his wife.
In planning this trip, we had chosen 'the dry',
as they called the dry season — one object: to drive
to Ayers Rock, the dead heart, the red centre, a place
of paintings and power, an energy source.
It could only be reached in 'the dry.' (In 'the wet'
the roads were impassable, rivers 'came down'
like wolves on the fold — a pack of them, fierce!
Dry riverbeds, suddenly swollen by rain,
made travel impossible.)
                    So much for plans!

It wasn't the season, but rivers 'came down'.
The Tod that divided 'the Alice' in two
rushed through like a train. Half the town was cut off.
The sluice gates above us had opened. Below,
rain's hostages, locked behind transparent walls,
we played cards and charades with our hosts and their young.
Not the reason we'd come, but a load of good fun.
And once the rain stopped we explored where we could,
bought boomerangs, bull roarers,[35] kangaroo knives —
guaranteed as *not* gammon, the genuine goods —

---

35 Ceremonial objects connected to male puberty rites.

and a sacred *tjurunga*.[36] Vague feelings of guilt
stirred somewhere within me, a foretaste perhaps
of the serious question of property raised —
how many years later? Concerns about voice
in addition to artifacts — stolen or sold,
or in some cases shared. Is a story not ours
whatever its origin? Some would say no.
I would argue the other side. Surely, we're one —
all peoples — mere twigs on a wide-branching tree.
Your story is mine, mine is yours, we entwine —
or so I'm inclined to believe. To believe?
That isn't the word — intuit's a much
more accurate choice. When we're sloppy with words
our world is despoiled. Or so I believe!

The airport was closed. No planes could get out.
Unless made of asphalt, the roads were awash
or worse than awash, were a-swamp or a-bog.
We went where we could, where we couldn't was most
of the countryside, half of the town!
But once, on a drive, coming over a rise
we frightened a flock of red-tailed cockatoos
which rose in a racket of scarlet and black
like feathery aircraft with gunfire and flak.

We attended the School of the Air, and arrived
at the station too early for school but in time
for the previous session of help for the sick —
heard the doctor on duty addressed by a dad
concerning his child. 'We are sending a plane,'
came the answer, immediate. How many miles
was that family from help? I dissolved into tears.
One weeps for oneself, I suppose. And I wept.

---

36 Sacred stone or wooden objects possessed by private or group owners together
with the legends, chants and ceremonies associated with them.

We were moved by the Outback, the manner of life
so different from Sydney's gold beaches and from
the grey stone of Melbourne; were moved by the lives
of the loners who lived their whole lives 'in the bush',
as we call it in Canada, wives who were wed
to a world full of men, to a loneliness hard
for us both to imagine, not primitive but
unexpected — that mixture of whites and of blacks
symbiotic, but, even so, light years apart.

*

The Royal Visit — for this, preparations took months.
Protocular knickers were tied into knots!
Untied and retied. Temper tantrums took place.
In addition, she came when the weather was hot —
Elizabeth, Queen, is the Royal I mean
a recent young queen, with her Prince as consort.
No disrespect meant, at the same time I'm not,
nor was ever, a Royalist, therefore for me
it was more of a romp than what James Reaney wrote
in his poem, 'Royal Visit', where everyone had
'a religious experience' (almost) in Strat-
ford, Ontario, three nine AD.

As for us, who were 'dips', we were groupies, or such
was our function — a cheering squad which
didn't cheer, but like lackeys attended events
dressed to kill, to the nines, to the I-don't-know-what!
New dresses, new hats, bejewelled, bejowelled.
Had the capital, Canberra, seen such a crowd?
Not since its inception — and not even then
when, no more than a pasture, it proudly became
Australia's centre of government as
the Duke of York opened its Parliament and
Dame Nellie Melba sang 'God Save the King'.

We practised our curtseys, 'Your Majestys', 'Ma'ams',
in case they were needed, and one wretched man
was so flustered he curtseyed when he should have bowed.
All the Cabinet Ministers' wives came to town
for this regal adventure of dinners and balls
and memorial services, speeches, parades.
Exhausting for us who were spectators, but
what the principals suffered, one only could guess.
Yet the Queen showed no symptoms of tension or stress.
Each hair was in place, each new outfit pristine,
word-perfect her speeches. A paragon queen.

*

New Guinea — Papua. Arthur was sent
to report on the area — was it, in fact,
developed enough for self-government?

                                        Now,
as I think of how little that world-wide white club
that *couldn't* or *wouldn't*, get into the skin
of naked black men who tucked flowers in their hair,
then I think we've progressed. We've at least understood
that we *can't* understand. Other people aren't us,
or let me reverse it: we aren't other 'men'.
Although, as I write it, I know it is true
only relatively — that *au fond*, we are one.

Port Moresby — as guests in the Governor's house,
with its shutters, high ceilings, slow fans, a black staff,
small bare-naked geckos said 'gek-gek-gek-gek'
(They talk with their tails, so I'm told. What a trick!)
to two bare-naked humans both dying of heat
in the bedroom, that is, although had our hosts said,
'chez nous, we dine nude,' we would both have said, 'Neat!'

An astonishing trip. It prepared us a bit
for the tropics (a posting we learned of in Lae

where our forwarded mail informed Arthur, 'Brazil.')
The flora, the temperature, roughly the same —
that was all, truth to tell. For New Guinea was not
the least bit like Rio! No more is it now
half a century later. Although it was hot
and humid and heavenly.
                              Flying we had
a close look at the land. Arthur's knuckles were white
but I, being ignorant, thrilled when we skimmed
the tops of the mountains in one-engine planes
and dropped into paddy green valleys and grazed,
like net shots in tennis, the tops of the trees.

One pilot apologized, saying, 'Once up
through that ceiling of cloud I'd have never got down
so I chose to stay low — although Hobson's! the choice.
And if you'd've undone your seat belts and budged,
the plane would have tipped, it was that touch and go.'

Goroka — the Highlands. I think it was here
the cargo cult started. At least it occurred
when white men arrived from the sky in a bird
dispatched by the islanders' ancestors and
jam-packed with provisions intended for *them*,
or so they divined. Who could blame them for that?
More logical far than the actual fact —
a machine made of metal that mastered the air!

To short-circuit this white interception, they built
a decoy on a hilltop to lure other 'birds' —
a contraption constructed of gasoline cans
and various trash — a travesty of
the most primitive plane, like the abnormal growth,
a tumour of hair and of teeth, I had read
about once. It had made me throw up.
I felt the same way seeing this. It was sick.
(Parallels with our culture are painfully clear.

Is the cargo cult merely a caricature?)

But back to Goroka. The Government man
with his wife and small child lived alone in the hills.
Their cook was a criminal hired from the jail.
He'd murdered his woman. A *crime passionnel*
was considered OK — his nature was known.
He wouldn't surprise them. They saw him as safe!
The devil you see, can in some lights appear
as an angel. Reverse it. It's equally true.
Believing is seeing. It's not in the eye.

For our welcome the tribesmen assembled, *en masse* —
half filling the valley — in war paint and plumes.
They were masked, they were tusked, and they stank to the sky.
Rancid pig fat for perfume — a filthier smell
you cannot imagine. They stamped and they yelled
like a furious beast, shook their sinister spears
at the sight of us. Let me assure you that this
was a welcome designed for the brave — O beware
all ye of faint heart, all ye lacking in faith.

There were orchids — all colours and sizes — from those
as large as your hand to small-fingernail size.
A thousand astonishments, details I thought
I would never forget have deserted like friends
who are faithless or dead. They have slipped out of sight.
A whole slice of my life — did it ever exist? —
that was glossy, rank-smelling, erotic, is lost.

What happened, I think, was that once we had learned
we were bound for Brazil, my thoughts flew ahead
imagining — what? I knew nothing beyond
Brazil nuts and coffee (though somewhere I'd read
of Carmen Miranda with fruit on her head!)
and the Latin American women I'd met
like flowers crossed with jewels. How could I measure up?

Brush the burrs from my hair, turn my pewter to gold?
A childish concern. Was I asked to compete?

★

Back in Canberra. Parties. Farewells. Packing up.
And more beautiful, now we were leaving, the light
and the carolling magpies high up in the boughs
and the silvery foliage of eucalypts, sweet-
ly scented magnolias, blackfellow trees[37].

When I think of it now, it comes back in a rush.
So does Lawrence, D.H., who had absolute pitch
in his book, *Kangaroo*. There he caught, on the fly,
in a matter of weeks, a flavour I'd missed:
bloody-minded machismo or machissimost.
This I had seen slant; he had seen it head-on.
It was part of their ethos, not much more than that,
but D.H. picked it up. He was radar equipped.

---

37 So named because from a distance they looked like naked Aborigines
brandishing spears.

VII

And so, back to Ottawa, thrilled at the thought
of family and friends.
          In a series of flights,
stopping briefly (our fate! we were never allowed
to see what we wanted) we set off for home.
Djakarta to Singapore then to Bangkok
Calcutta, Karachi, Port Said and Rome.
In England, a respite.
          Now, images merge:
muddy tropical rivers; and monkeys; and birds
flying into an airport and darning its air;
a breakfast in Egypt — red yolks to the eggs.
Michelangelo's Rome. And in London, Fonteyn.

When I saw her before, she had broken my heart.
And she broke it again. Some sense of a brink
she approached but stopped short of, some passion in check,
showed the tragic that hides at the heart of all art.

A telescoped trip. We were on the last lap.
I went shopping at Harrods and bought a red hat.

*

Canadians pale as white bread, plastic-wrapped.
I was stunned by the sight of us. Shock number one.
Number two — 'politesse', is a possible word
for evasiveness. Aussies would use 'insincere',
'hypocritical' even. I saw with their eyes.
And our accents were odd, once I heard with their ears.

No wonder External[38] plays musical chairs
with its diplomats. Leave them too long
and osmosis sets in. Over time they take on
another identity, even their look
imperceptibly alters. (Three years in Brazil
and I was Brazilian. Clothes maketh man.
Clothes maketh woman. And hairdos as well!)
'Born in an oven would you be a bun?'
a question my father would fling at his young.
I don't know about 'born in', but 'buttered' you would
willy-nilly belong to the world of the bun.

Culture shock is expected when travelling, but
culture shock coming home is a multiple shock.
I assumed — how absurd! — we'd return to the same
old landmarks and laws that obtained when we left,
but our country had changed, the time lag caught up,
and some transformations I hadn't foreseen —
bifocals or face-lifts for family and friends —
I managed to handle, but what I found hard
was I wasn't unchanged. An invisible ink
had written strange script on the page of my heart.

★

A month is too meagre for leave, let alone
to prepare once again for a future unknown.
Try shopping for cottons in winter. I spent
too much of my time in that fruitless attempt.
Giant cruise ships today take the rich to the south
so shops are well-stocked. You can buy when you wish.

---

38 External Affairs, the Department responsible for
diplomatic postings.

We bought Portuguese lessons on records and played
them whenever we could — in the shower, before bed.
I poured myself into the Post Report,[39] prayed
I could handle the house that was not only huge
but already the subject of chat. It was said
we were changing the chapel — the chapel! please note —
into, guess what? A bar. Not a word of it true.
We placed orders for foods to be shipped — this was part
of the ritual of going. Did Rio have none?
or was it that only Canadian food
was fit for Canadians? I didn't ask.
I followed the footsteps already laid down
in that as in other things. Hard to condone
how rapidly rebels comply and conform!
The Establishment smiles on quick studies and I
was a very quick study. I learned on the hoof.

I was brainwashed, I realize now, having read
both Sargant and Shah.[40] Having seen the technique,
I pray I'm alert to its methods and shan't
be brainwashed again — or a brainwasher be.
We have other dimensions, greater by far
than those our traditions require us to fill.
Overtired, ill-equipped, we set forth. My heart bled
once again for my mother. She didn't complain.
But I ached for her now that our roles had reversed —
and I ached for myself. Would I see her again?

The temperature plunged. Underfoot the snow crunched.
We steamed as we spoke. In the station the train —
holy smoke! — did its thing. Our friends saw us off
in their karakul hats with their runcible spoons,
all bundled and wrapped — a sea of fur coats.

---

39 A briefing prepared by External Affairs.
40 William Sargant's *Battle for the Mind* and Idries Shah's many books.

(How different today with our faux fur and down.)
Some noses were red, even dripped.
                              Then a spear
                              struck me through where I stood. I'd have fallen had not
                              a friend held me up. There were ghosts in that town.

Goodbye and goodbye and goodbye
                    and goodbye.

We sailed from New York on the S.S. *Brazil*.
Slow travel by ship gave us time to reflect,
be together again, and to read what we could
of this tropical country, its politics plus
its literature, history, geography — too,
to study the tongue we must speak to survive.
The fact that our teacher was Spanish was not
much help to our Portuguese! Nevertheless,
vocabulary-wise, we progressed, I would guess.

Dear Reader, you'll say I was spoiled. Well, I was.
We lived high on the hog, but we worked for our bread.
A kept woman I wasn't. I ran a hotel
for visiting firemen — all colours and stripes.
Down Under[41] was no preparation, for there
the house had been smallish, the servants were few.
The language was English. The customs I knew.
The prospects ahead were quite other: the house
was a Portuguese palace requiring a team
to polish its marble. The tongue, Portuguese!
And as for the customs — we hadn't a clue.
You could argue (I do) the whole thing was a farce.
A dying swan act, as the world falls apart.
Did I think like this then? I had questions of course,

---

41 Australia.

but, thrown in at the deep end, I swam to keep up.
As one of the last of those wives to accept
that their husbands' careers were their own, and because
you can write (if you *can* write) wherever you are,
I didn't rebel. It was grist to my mill.
But those younger than me were unsettled; they felt
a change in the air. Though they didn't conform,
they had not broken loose. They were aimless and bored.
While the next generation had lives of their own —
they were lawyers or physicists, pharmacists, pros,
career oriented, unwilling to go
as Third Secretary's women to any old place.

VIII

Our first glimpse of Rio we had from the rail —
a city of platinum and silver — the sky
heavy pewter, low-slung, with no sign of the sun.
The effect underwhelming. Except for the din.

Cariocas[42] are noisy, the racket they make
to Canadian ears is cacophonous — cries,
ghetto blasters and horns and loud laughter and shrieks —
like fire engines mating with monstrous machines.

The staff from the Embassy — *très comme il faut* —
were on hand to assist us. Like babes in the wood
that day we required all the help we could get.
Although Arthur — unflappable — would, on his own
have managed, I'm certain. But I would have flapped.

Through a chaos of traffic — four-lane and fast —
we drove 'home' to the Residence, entered through doors
as heavy and quiet as the doors of a vault.
Inside it was marble and flowers. Every flat
surface was covered with *cestas*[43] — the floor
likewise was covered. Extraordinary flowers!
And I wondered — a wedding? a funeral? or what?
The servants lined up — there were four, maybe five
if you counted the housekeeper (horrors! no hope
of *us* working together. I saw at a glance
Mrs Danvers[44] herself, and I dreaded the day
I would ask her to leave. While she, I would guess,
saw me as a pushover. I was too young.)

---

42 Inhabitants of Rio.

43 Flower arrangements, often in baskets, which is what *cestas* means in
    Portuguese.

44 The housekeeper in Daphne du Maurier's *Rebecca*.

The Embassy staff was on hand with champagne
and offers of help. But Rio in rain
is a body deprived of its soul, and the house
was a cell or a catafalque, cold as a tomb.
Low clouds for a view. The air a wet sheet
that clung to our skins.
                              When everyone went
we had showers — thanking heaven the water was hot —
in grey marble bathrooms with fittings of gold,
then we toured our pink palace — through elegant doors
of carved jacaranda. Reception rooms cold
as fish on a slab ran the length of the house.
Like headcheese in aspic, the pale marble floors
and the entranceway staircases. Outside, a pool
without water gaped empty — a hole in a tooth! —
although its proportions, of this I felt sure
were the rectangle, golden.
                              How give the place life?
Some paintings would help — Pegi Nichols,[45] perhaps,
better still some Chagalls, an enormous Bonnard
to flood it with colour. The walls were chalk-white,
the place smelled of mildew, the spaces were vast.

We went to bed early. The night was a loss.
There was firing close by, and although unafraid,
I thought, 'Revolution?' and Arthur as pale
as the moon in his nakedness, leapt out of bed
and onto the terrace the better to see
the gunpowder flashes. Who else in the house
was aware of the noise? Then the drumming began.
In the morning we learned that the 'gunfire' and drums
were a common event, every Saint had his Day,
every 'Day' had its ration of fireworks and fun.

----

45 Pegi Nichol MacLeod, a Canadian painter (1904–1949).

Arthur went to the office and I prowled about
in my cage. I was captive. Our car hadn't come
so I couldn't escape, but I unpacked and hung —
in my mind's eye — our paintings.
                                    The view was the same
as when we'd arrived — low cloud hiding all
but a candlewick lawn (we learned, later, each tuft
had been planted by hand in an intricate plan —
Burle Marx,[46] the designer, a setter of jewels).
But only a strip of it showed where I stood
on the patio, frozen, and longing for sun.

                      ★

Then one morning on waking the sun was a gong.
We rang with its light. What had died, was alive.
We had rings on our fingers and bells on our toes.
Dois Irmãos, the Two Brothers, twin mountains, arose
at the foot of our garden and stubbed the bright sky.
There were various palms, a stream and a pond
with lotuses growing. Anturias shone
in hot pink patent leather, day lilies — a wash
of gamboge against green. An impressionist's brush.

The house sprang to life. With the sun streaming through
five elegant transoms, five open French doors,
my heart was a kite, or, better, a bird —
for it sang as it flew. A woman in love,
I wandered entranced through rooms that before
were drab as a duster. I knew what to do.
Fire the housekeeper first. Once the jailer was gone
I could handle what came. And I did — and 'it' came!

---

46 Roberto Burle Marx, 1909–1993, one of the most prominent landscape
    designers of the twentieth century.

There were plenty of problems — the plumbing, the pipes
to the swimming pool. Wiring and phones!
Intermittent's the word for them. Sometimes they worked.
Then the inventory — heavens! — those pages of lists
of silver and crystal and china, things shipped
to furnish this residence. We were the first
Canadians in it. The job fell on us
to see that it functioned. Fruit knives and fish forks
and finger bowls — mercy! And facecloths that matched
with bath mats and towels. I counted and checked.

This, on top of the calls! The car came and went
with me, like a parcel, delivered, picked up.
Such opulent houses! Late wedding cake crossed
with early baroque. Or apartments that rode
out to sea like a barque, their view such a blue
I was dazzled, in love with the beauty, the bright
golden sheen in the air. A Dufy, a Matisse
wherever I looked. Then the city itself —
colonial buildings and those, *à la mode*,
that drew students world over — the sinuous curves
of poured concrete, the first. (Even Italy lagged
behind Rio in this.) And the *brise-soleils*[47] which
made intricate patterns of simple façades.

My vision was right for this rush of design,
correct for this colour — a visual thirst
quenched now by *that* column, *this* tree, a mosaic
of black and white sidewalks, a delicate spire.
Some deep correlation, unknown until then,
responded with yes and with yes once again —
a consummate bliss wheresoever my eye
chanced to fall.

---

47 Literally, sun breaks, formed by a perforated wall shielding the façade of the
building. A kind of decorative air-conditioning.

(This is far from the truth. To forget
certain things is impossible, even today,
some fifty years later — *favelas*[48]— in fact.
A congenital blindness afflicted the rich.
Those born to the purple had dye in their eye,
or so I concluded. How otherwise could
they have lived with the poor in their faces and paid
so little attention? Regrettably, now
I see in Canadian cities the same
disregard for the down-and-out. We have caught up!)

Back to beauty. Another dimension? Perhaps.
As the second's unreal if you know only one,
or the third is to 'flatlanders',[49] so is the fourth
nothing more than a fiction to those who know three.
Thus beauty — the fifth? — is a concept without
a perfect example. No flesh for a ghost
that some are in thrall to but others can't see.
Where does sightedness lie? In the heart or the soul?
Some say in the eye, but the eye, I suggest,
is really no more than an optical tool.

The sea in its blueness, the mountains like thumbs.
Leblon, Ipanema ('The Girl from'), the famed
Copacabana,[50] a crescent of gold.
Whatever my sins, the ozone and sun,
balloon men, kite venders, the black boys who played
futebol for my pleasure against the pale sand —
dissolved them like sugar in coffee. I soared,
a kite on a string. But I thought I was free.

---

48 Slums or shanty towns built over many of the mountains of Rio.
49 See *Flatland* by Edwin A. Abbott.
50 Three famous Rio beaches.

We acquired a menagerie — monkey, macaw,
two parrots whose screams were pongee[51] being torn,
and a terrier (Welsh) with too heavy a coat
for Brazil. He was charming when in his right mind,
and would greet us with presents, a leaf or a stick
he had searched for with care at the sound of our car.
But a bipolar dog breaks your heart. He became
at times so morose he could not hear his name
and he looked like a man with his head in his hands —
a James Thurber[52] man, in the form of a dog.

I received the macaw as a gift — gold and blue.
Arara, we called him — or her — who could tell?
He could imitate me calling 'Arthur' so well
that Arthur would answer — a laugh for us all
except Duke,[53] the dog, who'd have killed him because
he spoke in a tongue only humans should speak.
So we kept them apart. It was trickier still
when the marmoset joined us. She would have been meat!

(Today, looking back, I can't help but recall
The Animal Family, by Jarrell, Randall.[54])

Benjamina, the marmoset, came from Belém,
Amazonas — or was it Manaus? — I forget.
A *macaco leâo*,[55] the tiniest lion,
with the face of a tragedy queen, although then

---

51 Raw silk.

52 Author and cartoonist for *The New Yorker.*

53 Pronounced Dooky.

54 A children's book in which a lonely fisherman finds first a mermaid, then an
abandoned bear cub and finally a baby lynx. Not without difficulty, they
learn to live together in his one-room house.

55 Literal translation: monkey lion. Actually it is a marmoset with a leonine
head.

we had not seen a hair on her leonine head.
She'd arrived at the airport, delivered by hand
as a parcel, a gift from Senhor Benjamin
whom I'd met at a dinner the previous night
(our host, a drug lord, we were later to learn,
and were frankly appalled. Would we be so today?)
Arthur's gift was less practical. His was a plank
of mahogany. This he refused 'with regret'!
A monkey is practical? I would find out.

Pressed into my hands as we boarded our plane,
was a circular box made of cardboard, a size
to hold chocolates, perhaps, or a specialty cheese.
It had air holes punched in it by pencil or pen
and contained the alarmed and enraged marmoset
who chittered and banged its small body about,
and refused to be comforted — nothing I did
could heal its heartbreak — bits of biscuit pushed in
through the holes in the box only drove it insane.

Then we dropped fifty feet, and our coffee cups flew
ceiling-high in the cabin. The marmoset too.
Women screamed — they were scalded by coffee, but worse
was a marmoset, flying and frightened and fierce.
In that instant we christened him B. Fledermouse —
the B. for his donor, Senhor Benjamin.

(You'll have noticed the mixture of genders. It's hard
when a creature is small, to determine its sex.
Just think of those kittens you've held overhead!
But we finally figured him female and then
she became Benjamina — for better. Or best.)

My courtship was clumsy. I ordered a cage.
At my touch she flew into the tiniest rage.
She was me, microcosmic! How could I not see
human rage, as observed by the gods, is absurd?

I grieved for her — little and lonely and lost,
refusing all food and complaining non-stop —
and desperate, thinking that animal warmth
might offer her comfort, I held her against
my hip though she hated me, bit at my hands,
would have killed if she could — but she couldn't! Instead
she discovered my pocket, thenceforward her song
was a small 'Ode to Joy'. She was making it clear
that a pocket was what she'd been chittering for.
I sewed her a hammock. She made it her home.

(It is strange to me now that I give her such space.
Disproportionate, really. The delicate bridge
that connects us to creatures could not be more frail
than the one that connected the jungle to me.

I've frequently marvelled how dogs that have slept
on my bed, shared my breakfast — once given a bone —
revert, become lions and tear at their prey,
wild animals suddenly. They have had years
of living with humans — domestic as plates.[56]
Benjamina, however, was born in the wild
and accustomed to life in a tribe. How could she
have adapted so fast? When I let her run free
she sat on my shoulder and groomed me for fleas.
A miracle. Was I her mother? Her mate?)

★

Life lived through a topaz. My memory is
of a beautiful garden, a swimming pool with
Olympic proportions in which the pink house
proudly mirrored itself. At night it was like

---

56 A reference to Edna St. Vincent Millay's 'that now domestic as a plate /
I should retire at half past eight.'

a birthday cake, blazing. Inside, chandeliers —
three Cassiopeias — lit three lovely rooms.
At the back was the *mato*,[57] a forest that flowered
with *ipês, quaresmas*,[58] incredible trees,
and shameless *marias*,[59] so named because she
would blossom wherever — a carpet of blooms.

I was happy enough. Ecstatic at times,
but my pen wouldn't write. It didn't have words.
(No English vocabulary worked for Brazil.)
I stared at blank paper, blank paper stared back.
Then, as if in a dream, the nib started to draw.
It drew what *I* saw. It was fearless — a child
approaching a fire not knowing it's hot
yet not being burned — a miraculous child.
Every leaf, every flower, every table and chair,
the patio railings, the plants in their pots —
I had only to stare, intently enough,
and the pen did its careful, indelible work.
Encouraged by Arthur, returning with rolls
of exquisite paper tucked under his arm,
I learned about paper, its tooth and its weight.
And discovered with joy that my nib as it drew
sang a song as seductive as — now, I'd say Glass —
Villa-Lobos, I'd likely have said in Brazil.

★

Transformation. I changed. Someone in me was new.
Like an onion I seemed to shed skin after skin
or, more like a chart I had seen as a child

---

57 A natural forest.

58 The first, a yellow flowering tree, the second, purple flowering and named
    after the word for Lent, because that was when it bloomed.

59 We call it *impatiens*.

of the bodies — ethereal, astral and gross.
Fewer clothes. I felt free. Some connection between
the salt and the tropical sun and the strange
objectivity found through the nib of my pen,
the knowledge of papers, the knowledge of inks —
even black inks are various — fugitive/fast —
to say nothing of sepias. Arie[60] said,
'Why give up an art that you know for an art
where you start from the starting point — over again?'
Then he looked at my drawings and said, 'I was wrong.
Keep on going. You know what you're doing,' he said.

So I drew. But I would have. Wild horses could not
have stopped me from drawing. I drew in my bed
(the government sheets can attest to my zeal!)
I'd have drawn in my shower with my waterproof ink
if there'd only been waterproof paper as well.
Obsessed is the word for it. It was as if
some alternate universe opened each time
I stared at an object until it stared back.
I took lessons wherever/whenever I could
and I learned you can learn only that which you know.
The fire must be laid and awaiting the flame.
(If you want a whole apple, you have to have half.)
So began an adventure, a life-long affair
that led me to colour, egg tempera, oil
and then to mixed media, where I am still.
I wonder today, looking back, if 'Brazil'
was destined to happen wherever I'd been.

(This opens a question too big for my mind,
and one that 'The Hidden Room'[61] tried to address.
I suspect there's a sphere where all possible things

---

60 Arie Aroch (1908–1974) well-known Israeli painter, ambassador to Brazil.
61 'The Hidden Room', a poem in my collected poems of the same name.

co-exist — like the Noosphere [Chardin]. Or perhaps
a hologram's nearer the concept I seek.
Or do I mean Borges' 'The Aleph'? Alas,
I clearly don't know how to formulate this!)

★

Skin colour. A subject I'd rarely addressed.
No blacks in Alberta when I was a child.
I'd known one black student who went to McGill
and one or two others in passing. But now
in Brazil, as a guest, I'd no choice but to learn
the ways of the country. In Foreign Affairs
there was nobody black. And Brazilians we met —
all were white, every one. But in staffing one's house
the rules of employment were plain: upstairs maids
must be white; and *copeiros*[62] who served us; the rest —
the cook and the laundress and cleaners could be
black, white or whatever — this way I found out
I was colour-blind — if I had not made a note
in a job interview, I could only recall
a general impression — not colour of skin.
You would have to be born in Brazil to decode
the complexities colour presented. White skin,
the whiter the better, was prized by the rich
and so they avoided the beaches and bought
pearls that were darker than those we would buy
to make their skin lighter. Yet at the same time
they were proud of their blood. One Brazilian, when asked
how they handled their 'problem' replied, 'Marry it' —
she was blonde as Monroe, blue eyes and fair hair,
and to further confuse her poor questioner, said,
'My grandmother, God bless her sweetness, was black.'

★

---

62 Waiters.

How describe Ouro Preto (Black Gold), a small town
in Minas Gerais? And how come I can't,
as a writer, find words? It is surely my job!
Three hundred and sixty-five churches, I'm told
— the guilt of those gold diggers paying their dues
to a God who'd been good to them. Gold leaf galore.
String orchestras played holy music — baroque,
Brazilian baroque — in that dazzle of gold.
Colonial buildings and cobblestone squares
and burros with paniers, patient as posts.
Not much had been changed, but a modern hotel,
its façade, avant-garde — was a curious twin
to colonial buildings. Niemeyer[63] had found
some similitude, something that matched, some strange kin —
proportion, perhaps. Though the style was his own,
the whole was homogenous, some hidden law
underlay old and new and co-sanguined them both.
Inside, the hotel was another affair!
This architect's feeling for form was unmatched
by his feeling for people. Could he have cared less?
For instance, the bathroom: you wanted a shower —
but the shower-head was over the john. I don't joke.
It's the truth — the whole truth. Try imagining it!
OK, so we managed. And now we were dressed
and ready for coffee. The staircase that led
from the kitchen below to the dining room — hey!—
was narrow and wrought iron and spiral and steep.
There, one at a time, like a line of black ants
weary waiters with trays struggled upwards with food,
small Sisyphuses in recurring ascent
like the miners before them who'd struggled with gold

---

63 Oscar Niemeyer, a famous Brazilian architect who designed the new capital,
Brasilia. When someone asked President Kubitschek why all the government
buildings had subterranean entrances, he replied: 'Because my Michelangelo
has the soul of an armadillo.' (my translation)

while their masters grew fat overhead. It repeats,
this image, as if it were programmed. Perhaps
on this planet, 'Shikasta',[64] it has to repeat.

★

Boa gente — Brazilians. Their humour, absurd —
surrealist, even. Their poets were good —
Pignatari — concretist, de Campos and bro;
de Andrade, Bandeira, Mereiles. (Unlike
Australian poets who'd somehow got stuck
with Georgian diction — although they made up
with a leap once the time lag removed the iamb
and the models were changed. Why is it we must
have a pattern to follow — why is it we can't
hear the sound in our ear — our own sound? I think back
to Canadian painters who painted like Brits.
Conditioned by Constable, how could they know
the width of our landscape, the height of our sky
or the colour, when they had been brainwashed to see
a soft English landscape — grey, cloudy, with sheep?
So, when Seven, the Group of, portrayed what they saw —
they were vilified, laughed at by those 'in the know'.
Till the paradigm shifted, few others could see.)

I've digressed a long way. Back to poets, Brazil,
and though no *brasileira*, to Bishop, who lived
in Petropolis — nearly a neighbour, in fact —
whom I wanted to meet, and whose work I'd admired
ever since *North and South* had appeared and 'The Fish'
had rainbowed my room. There she was, within reach,
and I was too shy to approach her, for which
I have kicked myself since. It was silly. I think
it was talent that awed me, much more than crowned heads.

---

64 The title of a Doris Lessing novel — and a name for our earth.

Those I took in my stride. They were part of the job.

The painters. For me, Portinari and Di
Cavalcanti[65] wore crowns. There were others, of course,
and some days, in full sun, the salt air seemed to paint
the sea and the sky, every leaf, blade of grass.
The world was a painting, and I was a part.
Entranced is the word, or ensorcelled perhaps.

As to theatre, what patrons more faithful than us?
It accustomed our ear to vernacular speech
and our eye to depictions of popular art.
The plays were outrageous, tore strips off the Church,
in the fifties performed an abortion on stage
when abortions weren't legal. Authorities winked.
Girl Guides in blue uniforms ushered us in
and sold us their cookies! Was this a bazaar?

★

Surprises wherever we went. In the south
bull's semen and *maté*;[66] *fazendas*[67] and art
in the State of São Paulo; while up in the north
macumba[68] from Africa, brought by the slaves —
their Virgin, a sea goddess, Iemanjá;
the markets — Belém and Bahia were best —
a bewildering jumble of love charms, and fruits
only Goethe could recognize through his *Urpflanze*,
or 'theory' of plants. (It is like Necker's cube.
I catch it, and lose it. From right lobe to left?
I am handicapped, one-eyed, unable to hold

---

65 Candido Portinari (1903–1962), Di Cavalcanti (1897–1976).

66 A kind of tea.

67 Farms.

68 A form of worship.

what my third eye has glimpsed. Did I dream that I knew?
Holistic and linear jostle for space.)

In Belém we ate turtle — its shell was the plate.
(Why was it disturbing when oysters are not?)

And then to the famed Opera House in Manaus,
where Patti[69] performed at the height of the boom —
in rubber, that is — now a relic, a ruin,
a dowager building still wearing its jewels,
and where, on an untuned piano, we heard
a polonaise played for our pleasure. Oh please!

★

Up the Amazon. In a sternwheeler, wood-fuelled.
The captain and crew in impeccable whites
were smart as the Navy, all polish and spit.
The guests — what a gathering! — 'Cobley[70] and all':
the Mayor of Manaus, with his daughter and wife;
a Military Aide, much betasselled — and who
was a sleight-of-hand artist; the Chief of the Police
with his sister and sons; several Consuls; a slim
on-duty reporter; a dentist; and us.

The first night of our cruise we played cards — *vingt-et-un*—
until late, many laughs, much good humour, and tricks
from the Military Aide. Instant friendships were made,
short-lived, but immediate — love *à la carte* —
a Brazilian specialty, even an art.
They'd forget you tomorrow, perhaps, but today
you were kith if not kin — kissing uncles and aunts.

---

69 Adelina Patti (1843–1919), coloratura.
70 Of Widdicombe Fair fame.

At two in the morning we tottered to bed
in the VIP cabin — two bunk beds of straw,
a foot shorter than us, and a basin, pint-sized
for mini-ablutions. The toilets and showers —
there was one for the ladies and one for the men —
you imagine the rest!
                              We ate breakfast at six.
In the dining room — washbasins all in a row
where faces were washed and false teeth taken out —
there were two sides of pork and a quarter of beef
that hung from iron hooks. And alive, on the hoof,
a larder of milk mooed below us — six cows!
There were also two pigs (for fresh meat, we supposed,
but preferred not to think about). Hourly at night
we pulled in to shore to cut food for the cows
and wood for the engine, by starlight and flares.
It was beautiful, like an old painting — dark paint
with multiple glazes, astonishing depths
like the depths in a Rembrandt, the water with lights,
the skies overhead, the stars close, and the sweet
scent of cut grasses, the grasses themselves
brought aboard through a blackness as tactile as soot.

I'd imagined the Amazon — what child has not? —
it was one of the rivers we learned of in school.
I'd imagined the parrots and monkeys, the trees —
a real jungle, lianas. And what did we see?
The shore line was scrub. No monkeys. No birds.
A new kind of jungle, but nevertheless …
We were hot, sleep-deprived, and a little bit high,
yet the trip was a triumph, a total success.

★

'*Divino Espírito Santo* — a prayer
to the soul of your soul' — so a friend of mine said.
'If God is too big for you, pray to the good,

or the highest within you.' She wanted me saved.
Brazilians were Catholics — the women, that is.
I would say superstitious. They punished and praised,
were bullish or bearish to saints, offered bribes
to get what they wanted — emotional wants —
or so they appeared to the pagan in me.
I hadn't a god, but I know, if I had,
I wouldn't have bartered and bargained. Belief
at this primitive level seemed childish and yet
the Holy Ghost caught my attention, I'd heard
the rush of the air through its wings — starry air —
so when in Alcantara (northern Brazil)
in Canada's honour small schoolchildren sang
and two black women danced with silk flags and I asked
what the dance was about — the Archbishop replied,
'*Espírito Santo*,' and almost before
I had taken it in, I was breathless and blind
in a whirl of silk flags soft as feathers and wind.
'*Espírito Santo*,' the Archbishop said.
'They are giving It to you. Receive It,' he said.

★

I don't people my canvas with family and friends.
You might think I had none. Far from true. I had both.
Three very good friends who were friends till they died
Helena — Brazilian *da gema* — [71] with whom
I painted and drew. She might have been good
if she hadn't been rich. Big money restricts.
She was slave to her husband and grandchildren, slave
to her charities, slave to her role
as society hostess, her servants, her house.
But what she adored was to pack up her pens
and her pencils and paper and set off to sketch.

---

71 Native-born, literally, 'from the egg'.

And Trixie, pint-sized Panamanian. She
introduced me to Fonteyn who came to Brazil
to dance with its national ballet and brought
Michael Soames for a stunning, breath-stopping *Giselle*.
I spent a whole day with them both — on the beach
and in bistros. Believe me. Unlikely? But then
one's life *is* unlikely — no question of that.
I had seen her before. She had danced a *Swan Lake* —
both white swan and black. It had broken my heart.
The upshot of this was that when in Brazil
we met for the first time, I felt that she knew
my most intimate secrets — the same way one feels
when one dreams of a person, a person one knows
only slightly — if that — and when you next meet
the relationship's altered, for you, not for them,
and you feel you are friends. Some new threshold's been crossed.

The third was an artist. My teacher. He taught
me the stuff of his world. I took in what I could.
He had charms from the market and Paraná[72] cones,
clay dolls from the north and carved *figas*[73] of wood
and he played early music — Brazilian baroque —
and led me in ways I'd not ventured before.
'Dream a little,' he said. 'Your pen's full of dreams.'
He was right. And I dreamed. And the dreamer awoke.

And then I had Arthur. We worked as a team,.
complemented each other. Jack Spratt and his wife.
Like a Latin he figured that time was his friend —
an elastic commodity. I, even now,
think time is my enemy (placing the blame —
for blame must be placed! — on my parents' belief:

---

72 Beautiful cones from the Paraná or Brazilian pine.

73 A fist, with the thumb between the index and middle finger is a symbol of
    good luck in Brazil but in Europe considered blasphemous.

punctuality's second to cleanliness — thus
I learned it the way I learned cleaning my teeth).
So if *I* was upset when guests didn't arrive
at the hour they were asked, *he* could not have cared less.
The *hora inglesa* meant nothing to him.
We struggled with Portuguese, started each day
with a lesson. Those verbs! In colloquial speech
the subjunctive was used — future, present and past! —
an almost impossible, elegant tongue.
As a 'mouth', I spoke more. I was fluent but wrong,
while Arthur read better and could, in a pinch,
make a speech off the cuff — key words made to fit
the occasion's demands. He was clever at it.

And talking of speeches — when asked to address
the Brazilian Academy, based on the French,
a room of grey-bearded professional men —
I addressed them in Portuguese (written and read!)
with quotes from their poets, and brought down the house.
An astonishing act, nine parts terror, one — text.
Arthur's face when I singled it out in the crowd
was as bright as the sun in midsummer. He shone.

★

When our posting was up and we started to pack
for — where? — the UN in New York, for a start —
I hardly could bear it. How leave such a house?
Worse than leaving my friends. We would write. We might meet
at some future date. But the house? — such a loss!
We had made it our home, we had filled it with light,
with paintings and flowers. Made its chandeliers shine,
and its marble and wood. I had felt it was mine.
Now the truth was brought home. It was lent to us, like
all material things. (Shades of Bishop,[74] again.)

---

74 See her 'One Art'.

Ours to have, ours to love, ours to lose. And forget?
It was that I found hard. I could never forget
such a golden existence, such beauty? and yet
I quite possibly would. Life erases a lot.

(But I haven't forgotten. Those years were as near
to perfection as earthlings are likely to get.
Not perfect, of course. This planet is flawed,
along with its people. The apple has worms.
But living there, I was italicized. Some
curious alchemy altered my font.)

IX

New York. The UN. An East River hotel.
A suite meant for one, into which we both squeezed.
I lived in the galleries — the MOMA, the Met
fell in love with El Greco and saw *La Grande Jatte*[75] —
in the flesh, as it were — unexpectedly small.
It's a mystery, scale. There is magic involved.
And the Klees, I had known reproductions, of course,
but no matter how skilful, they couldn't convey
his extraordinary surfaces — concave, convex.
Some seemed to be bandaged with cheesecloth as if
the painting were wounded. A painting in pain?
(I found pleasure in matching initials — 'PK'.
We do grasp at straws! But coincidence is
a matter worth mentioning. What does it mean?)

At the Art Students' League and Pratt Graphics I tried
my hand at engraving and etching and learned
that although they intrigued me — the tools of the trade,
the burins and needles, the hard and soft grounds
the plates and the presses — the *process* itself
was too far removed from the final result.
There was always a plate between me and the print
and I wanted a contact much closer than that.

Through Marian Willard[76] I managed to meet
Charles Seliger,[77] one of her stable, who gave
me a lesson a week. His meticulous work —
organic, molecular, miniature —
today is renowned. He showed me techniques —
ways of doing, not seeing (we saw with one eye),
how to find the right pens, the right brushes, right inks.

---

75 A painting by Seurat.
76 Of the Willard Gallery.
77 American abstract expressionist.

And, he offered this pupil a pearl of great price
when he emphasized water and oil never mix.[78]

★

When Arthur was free of committees we went
to the ballet, and once — by astonishing luck —
for we took what we could, never booking ahead —
saw Brahms' *Liebeslieder* (the *Walzer*) in which
the musicians performed on the stage, just as if
they were in an Edwardian ballroom, and four
swallowtailed couples were waltzing beneath
chandeliers — did I dream them? — wall sconces perhaps.

When I count the events in my life that stand out
(theatrical, that is) then that must be one.
Gielgud as the Dane; Markova's[79] *Giselle*
Paul Robeson's *Othello*; and Fonteyn's *Swan Lake*;
all Tudor's[80] ballets; *Pericles* — Jean Gascon's
Stratford production that magicked us all;
The Dream Play with puppets at Tarragon; plus
The Thief of Baghdad — I was eight when I saw
that miraculous movie — my first silver screen.

And I ask, was it that that conditioned my eye
to Arabian images — mullahs? And mosques?
No, I'm not a Muslim. (Nor Christian, nor Jew,
come to that!) But since childhood my eye has been caught
by Moorish designs, by repeating mosaics,
and scripts — the Bihari, the Kufic, the Mashq —
that certainly must have affected my art.
'Calligraphic', they call it — or some of them do.
(Small wonder I saw in Abe Klein's 'Second Scroll'
a world I half knew, the obverse of my own.)

---

78 A principle that can be used to great advantage in painting.

79 Alicia Markova, prima ballerina with the Ballet Theatre.

80 Antony Tudor, choreographer of *The Lilac Garden, Pillar of Fire*, etc.

✗

Our next posting — Mexico. This time I packed
with a heavier heart. A new language. *Again*
that protocular dance! How repeat and repeat?
Point three, three, three, three. Like Eternal Return.
But when I could see, once my eye was engaged
(thank God for my eye, my insatiable eye —
it has seen me through much) then my mind was engaged.
And it wasn't Brazil-only-uglier as
I had feared it might be. It was clearly itself.
It was dark — all those virgins whose hearts were cut out.
I was certain the soil was made black with their blood,
that the gods were dark gods and resented all whites.
Who wouldn't — post-Cortez — the conqueror, who
in the name of *his* God put a culture to rout?

This was no time for history, alas, for the house,
constructed from lava — a hideous rock —
grey rubble without and grey rubble within,
was in need of attention, a cook, and some paint,
and I was in need of some Spanish — precooked! —
for, in less than a month, Dief the Chief, our PM,
was to pay a State Visit with Olive, his wife.
A double acrostic for Arthur and all
at the Embassy — schedules and plans
and split-second timing for visits and cars.
For me, nose-to-grindstone domestic affairs —
a functioning house full of lightness and flowers
with a staff that could handle the pressure, I hoped!
When we left for the airport I prayed I had not
forgotten some detail — had made myself clear
in Spanish, God help me, to those in whose hands
we now rested.
        Would someone be there at the gate?

Would the *moços*[81] remember white gloves? Would the Press
be offered refreshments? Would? Would? Would? Would? Would?
Who would choose such a life? 'Not I,' said the Hen.

The airport arrival was splendid. Much Brass.
The Chief gave his greetings in Spanish — a speech
he had learned on the plane. It was painful. No chance
any Mexican listening could have made sense
of the jabber he made of their language. He joked
that his Spanish was almost as bad as his French!
(What a change has transpired. Politicians today,
post-Trudeau, can hardly, but hardly, have hope —
without French — of achieving Prime Ministership.)

While back at the ranch, our staff had contrived
to do us up proud. They'd devised their own plan —
not one we'd have chosen, but nevertheless ...
A Canadian flag had been hung like a rug
from the mezzanine railing, with crepe-paper flowers
festooning the stairway. By chance there were no
mariachis to greet us — or fireworks — or both!
Unorthodox, surely, but how could we fault
such a sense of occasion, fiesta, in fact.
'Not I,' said the Hen. 'Cock-a-doodle,' said Cock.

Then the maelstrom began. (We had done this before
in Brazil — Sydney Smith from External Affairs,
and his wife, and his staff — a State Visit, in fact.
But when they arrived we were settled enough
to know who we were — even more, what was what!
There were crises, of course. The night that we gave
an *al fresco* dinner for fifty, a storm
blew up without warning. We barely had time

---

81 Houseboys.

to move the place settings inside when it struck
in great lashings of rain, a wild wind, a near flood.
And a blackout! Good God! Candlesticks to the fore
and flashlights and candles. We dressed in the dark.
'They'll be late; no Brazilian is ever on time.
They'll have no light to dress by. Our road will be out.'
But, eight-thirty for nine, they arrived. On the dot!)

Receptions and speeches, and meetings with top-
ranking officials, the press, photo ops.
And an escort of police. Look at me! Here I come!
Each siren is just like a shot in the arm
for, the truth is, this poor little biped is quick
to assume he is special — just give him the chance!
Is an escort of police not sure proof I'm a prince
or a princess — whatever? Red carpet rolled out
is never rolled out for the plebs and the proles.

Was it really important? We thought that it was.
Or did we? Important to do what we must
as well as we could. But we couldn't have thought
a world change was imminent.
                        As for the Chief
I suspect he was sure every word that he spoke
was of utmost importance. A petulant man,
and paranoid too. But enough is enough.

                  ★

The State Visit over, my life could begin.
(Though *that* was my life — heaven knows! But I lived
two lives, maybe three. Of the lives that I lived
I loved, without doubt, the official life least.)

We awakened each morning to sun! What a dream.
The air at that height — diamantine. And there

on the brilliant horizon — *El Popo*[82], snow capped,
a clone of Mt. Fuji's miraculous cone.

A whole land to explore. Looking back, what I loved
above all, were the villages fashioned from dust —
so it seemed to a newcomer — bricks from the soil,
grey on grey — and maguey,[83] the same colour — from which
they made *pulque*, that milky intoxicant, plus
their needles and thread, or so we were told
by an Aztec we knew. But no Aztec we knew
ever sewed with maguey. They had sewing machines!

The markets enthralled me. In stall after stall
huaraches, and sandals made out of old tires,
and glasses from Coke bottles, amphoras of
near-Grecian proportions, embroideries and
rebozos,[84] *serapes*,[85] astonishing toys.
The folk art might all have been made by a child —
uninhibited, funny, high-coloured and *right* —
as if from some other dimension where sight
made light of all preconceived concepts.

                                            Carved combs
were proudly displayed, as if equal in skill,
to Oaxacan black pottery, copper work, tin
candelabras and angels, bright bracelets and rings
of Mexican silver — the list could go on!

There were love charms, of course — hummingbirds wrapped in silk.
And snake oil for tapeworms, for tumours, toothaches —
all aches, come to that. Superstition and herbs
played their part — an immense paramedical part —

---

82 The familiar name for *Popocateptl*.

83 A common cactus.

84 A woven cotton shawl worn by the women.

85 A woven wool blanket worn by the men.

in a culture where church, the dark gods of the past
and those innocent virgins whose hearts were cut out
to appease these dark gods, all still struggled for power.

And each had its magic. Once entered, the church
overwhelmed you with incense and statues and gold
where the Virgin, dressed daily in silks and brocades,
owned a fortune in jewels that were changed with her clothes.
At a kiosk, outside, from a seller, black-clad,
you could purchase, for *pesos*, naive silver hearts,
silver eyes, silver legs, silver arms, silver feet —
to please a divinity. Bargains were struck.
The Huichols[86] made 'god's eyes',[87] a focus for prayer.
The peyote they picked was consumed to connect
to a Higher Community — capitals mine.
Their embroidery was fine. Their wool pictures inspired
by hallucinogens. Their bead pictures, bead bowls
were blinding with colourful images of
mythological beings — both antlered and winged.

On the Day of the Dead, the whole countryside reeked
of African marigolds. Acrid and rank,
that singular pungency, one that the dead,
it was said, were not deaf to — it guided them back.
The cemeteries blazed with great nuggets of bloom
piled high on the gravesites where relatives sat
to feast, and get drunk with, and talk to their dead.
(How different *our* customs! We dress our kids up —
'Trick or Treat' is the password — and send them to beg.)

Confectioners fashioned from sugar white skulls
and *panes de muertos*, the bread of the dead,

---

86 Indians from the Sierra Madre.

87 Coloured wool on bamboo frames and popular
    with the hippies.

while skeletons stirred from their closets, or rose
like spooks from their coffins and rattled their bones.
(Was Webster[88] a Mexican? Maybe he was.)

How talk of the pyramids? Monte Alban
a green and gold city, and Mitla's white stone
like drawn-work in linen — a detailed mosaic.
Palenque, Tikal — in the jungle — pale ghosts;
Uxmal (Yucatan) and Chichén, they were all
that remained of great cultures — their beautiful bones.

And then there were painters — contemporary ones.
Diego Rivera, Orozco and all
those painters of murals — Siqueiros — those men
whose work I *had* liked — (I had seen a large show
in the forties) but funnily, breathing their air,
I liked them much less. They seemed crude and grotesque —
propagandists, not painters — cartoonists, perhaps.
But Kahlo and Varo and Carrington[89] these
painters were *painters*. Tamayo *tambien*.[90]

Leonora-incredible-Carrington was
both angel and devil, a modern-day Bosch.
Her view of the world was a wonderful, weird
and beautiful nightmare. 'I paint what I see.'
And Varo — Remedios, masterful, more
symbolic than Carrington, both of them cut
from surrealist cloth, and both 'sisters' of Ernst.[91]
Formidable women — an eagle, a hawk.

---

88 John Webster, Jacobean dramatist. 'Webster was much obsessed
    by death....' (T.t]S. Eliot).

89 Frida Kahlo, Remedios Varo, Leonora Carrington.

90 Spanish for *also*.

91 Max Ernst.

Tamayo was Mexican. Anyone who
has been to Tabasco's Museum and seen
La Venta's giant heads[92] — baby heads, you might say —
would know him as progeny. He could have sat
as a model, in fact. And his paintings were part
of his heritage, history, his soil and his soul.
A painterly painter. I loved him the best —
or my eye did. The others I loved for the doubt
they cast on 'reality' — exquisite doubt.

Leonora, for me, was a gateway. She led
me to gesso's astonishing blindingness when
it's correctly applied (fourteen coats) and each one
so sanded and pumiced and polished they make
a surface like silk — a kind of divan
for egg tempera. Alchemy rather than art.
But art is an alchemy. If I had thought
it anything less, then I'd looked at some gross
simulacrum of art, or looked with my eye's
grossest body. (Refinement in looking is learned.)
And the medium?[93] — mayonnaise, actually — made
with an egg yolk, new laid, with no tincture of white;
for vinegar — turps; and for 'oliver' oil —
an artist's equivalent. This you could eat
in extremis, I think. It was kept in the fridge
and decanted as needed. It had to be fresh
then pounded with pigment, applied with a brush.

I loved it. The process, the way the ground sucked
the emulsion (or mayonnaise!), dried as you worked —
an intimate medium, wanting your touch.
Pearls gleam if you wear them and tempera too
comes alive if you rub it. I rubbed it by hand

---

92 Olmec heads weighing from ten to twenty pounds that resemble babies.

93 Egg tempera.

and then with a burnisher (nothing like oil
with its built-in 'Keep Off' and its mess to clean up).

Gold leaf. *Oro volador*.[94] Churches were filled
with its brilliance and glimmer. I searched for and bought
its frail little sheets, in their fragile square book.
I was eager to learn how to handle it, learn
how to lay it on gesso, co-join it with paint —
an art in itself, I was soon to find out.
Metaphysical? Maybe. A magical art.

Let me number the steps. Lesson one: with a brush
designed for the purpose — an 'eyelash' it's called —
pick up the gold leaf, but stop breathing, the least
exhalation will send the gold flying aloft.
And if, by some error, you *do* breathe, resist
the impulse to catch it, for there, in your palm
you will find a crushed clothes moth, the glitter all gone.

Lesson two: now stop breathing and try that again.

But before you stop breathing you have to lay bole,
a kind of red earth that's attractive to gold.
I'd forgotten this step! and I think I shall spare
you the process entire — it's a painstaking one.
The whole was breathtaking. Forgive me the pun.

★

You would think I did nothing but paint. Far from true.
We dined and were dined. We gave succour and drink
to troubled Canadian tourists — the robbed,
the mugged or the widowed or wounded. We went
to endless receptions. Occasionally met

---

94 Flying gold.

some visiting VIP — Nehru, de Gaulle,
Stephen Spender or Priestley,[95] or Jackie and John,
Mountbatten, or Tito, or Vivien Leigh
in town as 'Camille'. This list could go on
and would bore you to death. Name-dropping delights
other name-droppers only. I'm sure you're not one.

★

Was I ready for Mexico? 'Ready or not!'
we chanted as children. And such was the case.
One had to be ready—or be Aethelred.[96]
(What a joke! What a jester! Just who would have thought
I'd have dredged up from childhood the name of a King
I'd forgotten till now. Did I care for him *then*?)

★

I have said it before — if Brazil was the day
then night followed next. The dark night of the soul.
Not *losing* my god, I had none to lose —
but searching for one. I was brought to the boil
by what? Leonora and Gurdjieff and Jung
(the latter I'd read but was reading again);
archaeology, too, those great temples we climbed
and the gods they were raised to — the Sun and the Moon.

The 'mix' was unsteadying, urgent, and I
was at sixes and sevens (or was I at eights — [97]
infinity staring me straight in the face?)
The search was not new, heaven knows, I had searched
since birth, I suspect, via love, via art,

---

95 J.B. Priestley.

96 Aethelred, the Unready, King of England.

97 The figure 8 on its side — the lemniscate — is the sign for infinity.

via politics even — poor idiot me! —
a magnet in search of its mother lode, or
a chick for its hen? Incorrect, for a chick
outgrows its necessity, mine had increased.

Why Mexico brought me to this, I don't know.
A scrim was removed. Was this 'a thin place'?[98]
I read, as if driven. Teilhard de Chardin,
Ouspensky and Hammarskjöld, Huxley and James,[99]
The Cloud of Unknowing — the list could go on.
A promise of food was provided but none
appeared on my table — no crust and no crumb.
I was starving, despairing, when onto my plate
came, in typescript, my first introduction to Shah.[100]
Something in me was stilled. Some thirst was assuaged.

---

98 In Celtic mythology a place where the soul awakens.

99 William James's *Varieties of Religious Experience*.

100 Idries Shah (1924–1996) exponent of Sufism in the West.

XI

Arthur's term was now up; Mexico, our last post.
(This phrase, to a military brat, is a wound,
a wound with a plaintively suffering sound.
How many Remembrance Days during my youth
did the bugle sound forth for the military dead?
To a child it was almost unbearable — some
unimagined anxiety hung in the air
and shrouded November eleventh each year.)

This was different, no doubt, but the phrase by itself
has a sad, dying fall, as of time running out,
which it was. Bitter sweet. We were sorry to leave
companions and comforts but glad to be done
with formalities, protocol, pleased to go home.
I liked the idea of four seasons, a house
we could do with whatever we wanted, a base
from which we would journey, to which we'd return,
and of being plain Mr and Mrs again.

We decided to drive — to delay the splashdown.
Re-entry made easy — just us and the car —
no appointments to keep, no schedules nor quick-
change contortions, or cocktails and meaningless talk
(as a friend of mine said, It's OK for the men —
they have things to discuss. We must make subjects up!)
Those the prices I paid for the fabulous perks:
pre-Columbian wonders — a world in a world;
new flora and fauna and new kinds of fun —
jai-alai,[101] for example, a spectator sport
for us — to say nothing of sambas and surf.

---

[101] A Basque game played with a long racket on a three-sided court,
said to be the fastest ball game in the world.

But I longed for a slightly less disciplined life,
forgetting I wasn't the person who'd gone
abroad in the fifties. Back then I was young
I could cook, do the laundry, look after my house.
(Use it or lose it was never more true!)
And now, to my horror, I found I must learn
all over again. I was clumsy and slow
and, worse, I discovered — ashamed — I had grown
accustomed to privilege. How it occurred
I couldn't imagine. Seduced, is the word —
a gradual seduction — and I had succumbed.
Had I not been left-wing ever since I could vote?
Had I this? Had I that? True enough. But more true
was this middle-aged woman whom I wouldn't like
had we been introduced — How d'you do. How d'you do.

(Know thyself ...? Take the lumps. You are not who you think.)

★

Homecoming was hard. I'd forgotten how cold
Canadians seem. I was Latin by then
and demonstrative ways were not welcomed by friends
from my earlier days. I felt foreign at home.
All the warmth I had learned I must unlearn again.

It was like a new post, for we moved to the west
where neither belonged. It was beautiful but
unfamiliar and far from the family and friends
I had thought we'd returned to. But there, at long last,
we were once more united with Chico, our dog,
who'd been six months in quarantine, breaking three hearts.
He spoke Spanish, our Chico, a literate chap,
astonishing onlookers when he obeyed
commands in a tongue they could not understand.

Arthur worked at *The Times* as its publisher, thus

returning to newspapers. He had begun
as a junior reporter, then moved to *Maclean's*
where he'd searched for, and nurtured, a talented team
of fearless and accurate journalists — Blair
Fraser, Ralph Allen and Berton, Pierre —
to name only three. With him at the helm,
'colonial rag' became 'national mag'
and flourished and flowered. Is its day nearly done?)

We purchased a house with a peach tree, a pond
and a study apiece. At the front a giant fir
'enverticalled' us and its right-angled boughs
made lovely our living room, filtered the light
in patterns that changed with the wind and the sun.
(We little then knew that one night in a storm
it would measure its length on our roof. We were like
a bombsite — a rubble of concrete and glass.)

At the back there was bush — a bewilderment of
snowberry, oak and wild blackberry canes.
I could see at a glance from the way he surveyed
his property, all Arthur's pioneer blood
and land-clearing ancestors clamoured to act —
get a hatchet, a scythe and a pickaxe and make
from wilderness Eden. He would. And he did.
His garden: curved beds, winding paths leading to
hidden places, bright flowers in profusion, a hedge
to make his park private — a personal place.
(Today it is beautiful still. I have tried
to keep it that way — a memorial made
by his hands and his heart. I feel he is here
in the steps that he built, in the bushes and birds,
in the wholeness of nature. He needed to feel
the earth underneath him. The sun overhead.)

*

Those were good years and bad. Arthur watched with a gaze
as objective as God's the things that went on —
the Balkanization of Canada which
he feared our undoing. He wasn't far wrong.
Trudeaumania. TV. The fact that the west
so hated the east (once a westerner, you
understand why it happens — wherever you are
you grow one-eyed — a bigot). If only we could
add an eye we would have a Triclopian view:
not Federal/Provincial, but both of them, plus,
not English/Français, but the two — with a third.
The wholes being more than the sum of our parts.

Centennial Expo Six Seven, seemed proof
that we'd taken a leap — had acquired a third eye
that saw wider and further! Our planners conferred.
Doubting Thomases doubted, designers designed
and Expo resulted. The country rejoiced.
The Pavilions, the artists, the music, the mood
of the city were marvellous — Montréal sang.
The States built a dome — geodesic, goddam! —
and sixty-two countries took part in the plan.
'A great work of art!' someone wrote, and great art
makes you feel you are great and we took it to heart,
little knowing we'd peaked and, like Orson,[102] alack,
our great future ahead, lay behind, at our back.

                    *

When we sailed for Australia, poets were seen,
and, like children, not heard. Not that many were seen!
Home again, I discovered that poets were bards
paid to sing for their suppers — in colleges, schools

---

102 Orson Welles, about whom it was said that he was a young man with
     a great future behind him.

and bookshops — wherever. Some good, others bad.
Reading poetry well is an art in itself —
not one I had learned — so I dreaded the day
I might be invited to read. When it came
it was Purdy[103] who asked. He was at SFU
as Writer-in-Residence. I was to read
to the English Department — the students of Djwa,
Gordon Elliott, others whose names I forget.
(I can barely believe it today, but back then
I was awed by professors, assumed they possessed
more knowledge than I did [they did — and they do!].
But their knowledge was not what I thought it would be.
All I knew about college had come to me through
descriptions of Cambridge — my aunt, as a lass,
taking lectures from Whitehead and Russell, no less!)

I practised and practised before the event
in dread of the moment and then, on the day
I was scheduled to read, some voice in my head
said, 'It's nothing but ego. So what if you do
make a fool of yourself? Who will care if you do?'
and my nervousness fled and I rose and I read
like the man from Japan in the limerick[104] who
tried to fit it all in — a fast train going through!

I was writing again. I'd not written for years
except for a journal — not 'Journaling', just
recording impressions. No poetry, prose.
(For me prose was fiction, so facts didn't count.)

---

103 Al Purdy.

104 There was a young man from Japan
     whose poetry never would scan
     When they asked 'What about it?'
     He angrily shouted,
     'Yes, I know, but I want to get as many words into the last line as I possibly can.'

But now I was writing and drawing full tilt.
Had a show at the Art Gallery. Brought out a book.
Joined the League[105] and met poets and travelled a lot,
gave readings all over the country and once
with Ondaatje and Birney I toured the UK.
Saw the Lake Country, Grasmere, and Wordsworth's small house
where he lived with his sister. No cat could be swung
in such minuscule rooms — not a kitten, in fact.
Tiny windows, low ceilings. I thought of the winds
and the drafts of the winter, long hours in the dark
and remembered his lines on 'celestial light'.

I was active, still young (in my fashion), involved
in a number of projects. With Pat Martin Bates
remodelled a building (a dollar a year)
into studio space for young painters. One snag
was their planting of opium poppies and pot
on government property — not a good place!
But we opened the Signal Hill Gallery, a small
brightly painted, well-lighted, harmonious space.

We made puppets — hand puppets — and put on a show
with a prince (on a horse!) and a dragon (with smoke!)
and scene changes (three!) We were greenhorns and so
didn't know what was possible. No pro would do
what we, in our ignorance, dreamed up. And did!
(Thus empires are born. Pioneers, to a 'man',
have amateur status. All started from scratch.)

If I say it myself — I do say it myself! —
it was beautiful — scenery, costumes and script —
and music and magic — those special effects.
We drew a large crowd — we were such a large cast —
another mistake, but we managed. And when

---

105   The League of Canadian Poets, founded in 1966.

at the end, as our hero returned with his bride
and his countrymen crowded the rooftops and cheered,
the children went wild and the strongest men wept.

★

I attended the Adelaide Festival. This
was a total surprise! — the whole country, I mean.
Wool must have done well. The cities had bloomed —
fine theatres and galleries and restaurants — and now
this astonishing festival. Adelaide, once
no more than a town, was a city, in fact.
And an elegant one. She was truly a queen
in her Festival dress.
                        The White Policy[106] done,
the country'd cast off its provincial mien.

The Festival menu was gourmet, and more
than the greediest gourmand could possibly eat:
there was *Lady MacBeth del Distrito de Minsk* —
Shostakovich's opera; a play from Brazil;
and Rushdie and Hoban, Keneally and Hope[107]
and beautiful Chatwin,[108] and Françoise Gilot;[109]
and music from Europe (post-mod and Mozart).
A fabulous feast. An emotional lift.
(Is it coincidental that 'art' rhymes with 'heart'?)

★

Professionally, I had had a slow start.

---

106 The White Australian Policy that allowed in only white immigrants was
     done away with in 1973.
107 Salman Rushdie, Russell Hoban, Thomas Keneally, A.D. Hope.
108 Bruce Chatwin.
109 Author of *My Life with Picasso*.

In a world of confessional verse, what I wrote
was not *à la mode* — not *exactly* old hat —
nor was it post-modern. I didn't quite fit.
But I wrote. This and that. A memoir of Brazil;
children's books; a short story — apocryphal — that
Joy Coghill performed as a one-woman show
with Cram[110] on his flutes. My 'Collected' came out
(What an editor, Stan![111] What a bookmaker, Tim![112])

Then I found a new form and, inspired, at full-speed
wrote a bookful of *glosas* — the book, *Hologram*.
(Chronology here is askew. So what's new?)
And at Roy Thomson Hall, with the symphony and
massed voices, D. Holman's[113] big music was sung —
oratorio music — my poems the words.

The eighties and nineties were full to the brim —
new friends and surprises and honours (unearned).
And now in the twenty-first century new
forms have engaged me. I've made a CD
and written a one-act libretto (performed)
the music by Höstman,[114] completed this long
colloquial memoir, and finished a book
of nonsensical verse and my drawing board's up
and I'm drawing again. It's like eating dessert.

---

110 Robert Cram.

111 Stan Dragland.

112 Tim Inkster.

113 Derek Holman, composer, whose 'The Hidden Reality' was performed in the
     year 2000 at Roy Thomson Hall in Toronto with the Toronto Symphony
     Orchestra, the Elmer Iseler Singers, the Toronto Children's Choir and soloists
     Ben Heppner, Susan Platts and Wendy Nielsen.

114 Anna Höstman, a young Canadian composer.

XII

I write this today as the world falls apart —
two thousand and four, August first. It is hot,
not unseasonable — it is summer — but hot
for this northerly hemisphere; full of freak storms
and assorted disasters — floods, wildfires, and drought.

That's the weather report. One sign of the times.
There are others. They surface wherever I look.
Is it age or a sharpened perception that sees
world's end? Is it entropy doing its work?
What about the consumer society? What
is this grievous disgruntlement, feeling of loss,
that drives people shopping for things they don't want?

And obesity? Booze and junk food and TV
and cars and computers and junk food and beer
and cars and cosmetics and popcorn and pop
and junk food and chocolate and junk food and death.

Big is beautiful — so manufacturers think —
giant sofas in which the obese can feel thin
and glasses designed for the ham-fisted — too
tall for your dishwasher. Something's amiss.
Anorexia. Cancer. Bulimia. Angst.
Rice. Cheney. And Rumsfeld. And Ashcroft. And Bush.[115]
All modern diseases. From which we may die.

Is it God being dead? Is it greed? Is it drugs?
Is it all the above? Is it something beyond
our control, even if we'd a clue what to do?
Something cosmic perhaps, some part of a plan
our minds cannot grasp? Is it bad? Is it good?

---

115 George W. and his advisors.

How know good from bad? My vision is short.
The long body of time is beyond me. And space.
Are crop circles only a beautiful hoax,
or some other dimension entering this
three-dimensional world? A cross-section, perhaps,
of a many-dimensional happening? Where —
oh, now that we need him — is Goethe, gadzooks,
that fabulous 'looker' who looked with an eye
like an x-ray or laser? His theory of plants
B. Mandelbrot recently proved with his 'set'.[116]

I had somehow believed — a poor word that, 'believe',
when unthinkingly used — for belief implies fact —
so I hadn't believed but I'd hoped against hope
that a critical mass would up-tilt the whole mess,
align all our molecules, alter our sights
and save us.
        Alas! I can see no such thing.
'Things' only get worse — or such my dark view.

If Arthur were here he would tell me again
that this biped who sports an opposable thumb,
and survived thick and thin, will most likely come through.
He had a strong faith, not in God, but in man.
While mine's in a god I cannot second-guess.

I am out of my depth. What interests me most
is beyond me: the hologram, fractals and 'god'.
If I understood one I would understand all —
or so I imagine. I'm missing the gene
that could make it all clear. I can't enter the space
where discreteness dissolves and the many are one
though I dream of it often and if I can dream
that's perhaps the first step, for false gold can't exist

---

116   $x = x^2 + c$.

if there isn't real gold — a fact that's as plain,
once you've taken it in, as the nose on your face.

★

Though sickness and death take their terrible toll
and they did and they do — one's astonishing heart
almost sings through its grief like a bird — water bird —
in the wind and the waves of some vast salty sea.
Explain it? I can't. But it's true I'm in love
with some point beyond sight, with some singular star
for which words won't suffice, which reduce it, in fact.
Head on it's invisible, if I should look
with my cones, not my rods,[117] it would vanish — expunged;
if I glance to the side, through my rods, then the star
shines as brightly as Venus. Which truth is *the* Truth?

★

Nero fiddled. And fiddled. What else could he do?

Victoria, June 2005

---

117 Rods and cones are the light-sensitive photoreceptors of the retina.

P.K. Page was born November 23, 1916, at Swanage, Dorset, England. She left England with her family in 1919 to settle in Red Deer, Alberta. She was educated in Calgary and Winnipeg and later studied art in Brazil and New York. In the early 1940s Page moved to Montreal to work as a filing clerk and a researcher. She belonged to a group that founded the magazine *Preview* (1942–45) and associated with F.R. Scott, Patrick Anderson, Bruce Raddick and Neufville Shaw. Her poetry was first published in *Unit of Five* (1944) along with Louis Dudek and Raymond Souster. From 1946 to 1950 Page worked for the National Film Board as a scriptwriter. In 1950 she married William Arthur Irwin, who figures as Arthur in her later poems and as A. in her *Brazilian Journal*. She is known as a painter under her married name, P.K. Irwin.

P.K. Page has won the Governor General's Award (1954) for poetry, and has been appointed a Companion of the Order of Canada.